THE REFERENCE SHELF

Vol. 30   No. 4

REPRESENTATIVE AMERICAN SPEECHES: 1957-1958

Edited, and with Introductions
by
A. CRAIG BAIRD
Department of Speech, State University of Iowa

THE H. W. WILSON COMPANY
NEW YORK   1958

PREFATORY NOTE

REPRESENTATIVE AMERICAN SPEECHES: 1957-1958 is the twenty-first in this annual series. Each volume contains some eighteen "representative" speeches, by Americans, or by others who have talked in this country (for example, Winston Churchill). These twenty-one volumes include more than four hundred addresses by more than three hundred orators. (See the Cumulative Author Index for a full list of speakers and their addresses.)

Classification of speeches. As in previous volumes, the speeches have been grouped according to their subject matter, such as International Policies, Industry, Labor, Party Politics, Agriculture, National Ideals, Personalities, Education, Religion.

The Introductions to earlier volumes (for example, the 1948-1949 edition) have listed alternate classifications of the speeches, such as those before Congress, on the political stump, at labor conventions, in the court room, at university commencements, and on ceremonial occasions, including dedications and anniversaries; introductions of speakers; and radio or television speeches.

Selection of speeches. This editor disclaims his selections as the "best" of the thousands of important speeches of the year. He does attempt to single out those addresses that assume importance because of their ideas, organization, language, and delivery, and their reflection of major events and trends. Contemporary history, he assumes, is partly the product of the platform influence of leaders. But events in themselves call forth speakers who otherwise might remain inarticulate. Speakers make the times, but events also create the "voices of history."

The speakers chosen for these twenty-one volumes are a cross section of the different types. There are political speakers (the majority) but there are also effective representatives of business, labor, law, religion, education, and other categories.

Introductions to the volumes. The Introduction to each of the twenty-one volumes deals with some phase of the methods of communication, or outlines the leading movements of the immediate months and identifies the speakers with these events

and trends (for example, President Eisenhower in November 1957, discussing the Soviet Union's missile launchings).

Introduction to each speech. A short introduction to each speech is included. Brief background, occasion, chief ideas, language, delivery, and effect of the speech are sketched to provide further insight into the speech itself.

Biographical notes. Brief biographical facts concerning each speaker are listed in the Appendix. Readers are thus encouraged to examine background, personality, and speaking methods.

Table of Contents and Cumulative Author Index. These twenty-one volumes, with their individual Contents and the Cumulative Author Index, provide an excellent basic reconstruction of the important events in American history and affairs since 1937. The successive periods can be studied in detail: (1) the period prior to the Second World War; (2) the speechmaking of 1941-1951; (3) the debates and other speeches of the Korean war period; (4) the public addresses of the Post-World War II period, 1951-1957; (5) and the speechmaking of the space-atomic age after 1957.

A reference source. This volume, like its predecessors, is a reference source, useful for subject information and for speakers and speeches to be studied as types. Each volume, in addition to its use as a library reference, is suggested as an aid to students of discussion and debating, public speaking, history and criticism of contemporary American public address, and social sciences.

The editor is grateful to the various speakers and publishers for their cooperation in providing authentic texts and in giving permission for these reprints. Special acknowledgment is made in each case. The editor appreciates the cooperation of several university libraries and staffs, including Ralph Parker, Director of Libraries, University of Missouri, and his staff; Norman Kilpatrick, Director of Libraries, Florida State University, and his staff; John Sykes Hartin, Director of Libraries, University of Mississippi and his staff; the library staff at the University of Washington (Seattle); and especially Ralph Ellsworth, formerly Director of Libraries, State University of Iowa, and his staff.

A. CRAIG BAIRD

May 1958

CONTENTS

EDUCATION

RELIGION

INTRODUCTION

SPEECHMAKING AND CONTEMPORARY HISTORY

The effective speechmaker both influences and responds to his day. If "times of crisis are times of terror," they are also times that beget great speakers. How much the crisis itself is responsible for stimulating eloquence is problematical. The American revolutionary spirit after 1763 produced a coterie of persuasive statesmen. So did the later critical years when Lincoln, Wilson, and Franklin D. Roosevelt came to their highest oratorical expression. The question, on the other hand, of how far the speaker shaped the national attitudes and history is also debatable. In any case, the close link between public address and the social-cultural-political currents is obvious. American trends are interwoven with platform leadership. Cultural history, therefore, cannot be properly understood without proper analysis of the oral communicative force so active in that history. It is equally true that the student of speechmaking needs to take full account of the social background that in part determines or reveals the orator's thought, his persuasive appeals, his immediate and long-range effectiveness.

What are some of the major problems of 1957 and early 1958 that called forth particular types and trends in speech-making? [1]

INTERNATIONAL PROBLEMS

Space-Atomic Race

In October 1957 began the Space-Atomic Age. On October 4 the Soviets projected a satellite (Sputnik I), into the earth's orbit. This "earth moon" weighed 184 pounds, moved in an elliptical orbit at a peak altitude of some 560 miles, and circled the globe once every ninety-six minutes. On November 3 a

[1] For comparison, see the Introductions to *Representative American Speeches: 1955-56* and *1956-57.*

second Soviet satellite, weighing some 1000 pounds, soared 1000 miles into space (with a dog, Laika) and remained in orbit until April 1958.

Americans, scanning the October skies and hearing the "beep-beep," were startled, anxious, confused. American confidence in our scientific-technological leadership was apparently oozing. More specifically the Soviet space bodies proved clearly Russia's power to produce and project long-range intercontinental missiles. The day of the Western world's reliance on conventional long-range bombers for defense was apparently over.

American public speakers—Congressional leaders, industrialists, educators, scientists, and television commentators—became articulate on this topic. Senators, for example, castigated the Pentagon and the Eisenhower Administration for the missile-rocketry lag. Senators Styles Bridges of New Hampshire, Henry M. Jackson of Washington, and Richard M. Russell of Georgia, former President Harry Truman, and a long list of others chimed in to denounce or to exhort. Senator Stuart Symington, long a spokesman for greater air force support, in discussing "the significance of the Sputnik on American Defense Policy," pointed directly to President Eisenhower for our missile-rocketry tardiness. On November 4 Symington, in his address on "Time for Action," declared that "it is clear that the American people have been misled.[2]

Vice President Nixon, in a major policy speech before the International Industrial Development Conference, at San Francisco, on October 15, agreed that the satellite was not to be dismissed as a "scientific stunt," for "Russia has developed scientific and industrial capacity of great magnitude." President Eisenhower in a notable speech on November 7 attempted to reassure the nation and its allies, to promise unity and greater efficiency in national defense, and to indicate quick restoration of the military balance with Russia.[3]

The missile-rocket problems that America debated after early October 1957 concerned chiefly (1) our power to speed up space weapon production, (2) our ability to maintain the backing of

[2] For Symington's speech, see p31-5.
[3] For Eisenhower's speech, see p 19-30.

our allies, (3) our skill in offsetting the tremendous Moscow propaganda following the Soviet space launchings.

(1) How could the United States and its allies restore the military balance before all was lost? Should our military Defense Department be radically reorganized and unified? Should "czarist" authority be lodged in the chairmanship of the Joint Chiefs of Staff? Or in the Secretary of Defense? Or in some layman (like scientist James Killian, Jr.), armed with sufficient power, courage, and judgment?

Within the program itself should priority be concentrated on the Army's Jupiter, or the Air Force's Thor, or the Navy's Polaris? Was our productive lag due chiefly to an interservice competition for priorities and technical manpower? Or to inadequate budgets? Or to general complacency? And to downright lack of technical knowledge?

The successful firing into orbit of the first American satellite, the army's Explorer, on January 31, 1958, and the successful launching of two additional satellites went far toward restoring damaged American prestige.

(2) In developing such a costly Intercontinental Ballistic Missiles and outer space program, should the national debt be increased? If so, how much? And in the over-all national spending should agricultural subsidies, foreign aid, educational supports, and similar expenditures be cut?

(3) How could the United States ensure the continued military-economic solidarity of its allies? Should NATO nations be persuaded to become bases for ICBM weapons? Would Congress vote for our sharing atomic secrets with NATO allies? President Eisenhower and Secretary John Foster Dulles at the Paris meeting in December 1957 proposed measures for close NATO cooperation. Later these two reported to the American people optimistic results of their Paris deliberations.

(4) How could the United States offset the Soviets' increased propaganda drive? Their psychological maneuvering, 1958 style, aimed to impress all, especially the Western world, with Russia's military might; to trumpet simultaneously "peaceful coexistence"; and to woo the neutral and underdeveloped nations

of Africa and Asia by promises and economic commitments, totaling since 1955 "more than a billion dollars."

Specifically, the Bulganin-Khrushchev propaganda by letters, speeches, and vodka conversation, spelled out their aims and methods: to weaken the fifteen-nation NATO pact in Europe; the eight-nation SEATO pact of Southeast Asia; the five-nation Baghdad pact of the Middle East; and incidentally—thus far— the twenty-one-nation Organization of American States. These pact members were in turn warned against destruction in war and exhorted to peace and neutrality in the Russo-American power struggle. The Afro-Asian People's Solidarity Conference in Cairo at the year's end, under Russian influence, had all the trappings of an "African-Asian Cominform."

Two major aspects of this propaganda barrage confronted Washington and the nation and compelled decision: (1) Moscow's repeated demand for a "summit conference," and (2) the accelerated economic and technological undergirding by the Communists of vast territory in Africa and Asia.

Should we approve of a summit conference in 1958? The pressure from Moscow, echoed by Britain, and by many thinkers in this country, was great. President Eisenhower, with the memory of the futile Big Four Conference at Geneva of July 1955, refused to rush into what would probably be a fresh sounding board for Soviet disarmament proposals on their exclusive terms.[4]

Should the United States counter the new Soviet economic and political advances in Egypt, Syria, and elsewhere in Africa and the Far East, by our own increased mutual aid? And should we lower tariff barriers and extend the reciprocal trade agreements? On these issues of foreign aid and tariff policies, Adlai E. Stevenson, Justice William O. Douglas (urging economic aid for India at Columbia, Missouri, in December 1957), Clarence Randall (at Detroit, December 9, 1957), Senator John Sparkman (at New York, December 5, 1957), and many another talked as the Eighty-fifth Congress, second session, 1958, prepared to debate these issues.

[4] See *Representative American Speeches: 1955-56*, p 19-24, for Eisenhower's speech at Geneva.

Hungary

The suppression of Hungarian liberty was a stark reminder of the survival in 1956 of ancient barbaric ruthlessness. Hungary's revolution, beginning on October 23, 1956, was crushed by Soviet tanks and troops. Thousands of Hungarians were killed or rounded up and shipped to the Soviet slave camps. Other thousands managed to escape to the free West.

The free world was revolted at the spectacle. The United Nations condemned Russia for this rape of a nation. An investigation, in which the details of the Soviet brutal record were documented, was reported to the General Assembly in June 1957. On September 10 the United States chief delegate, Henry Cabot Lodge, Jr., spoke for adoption of the report.[5] It was approved by a vote of sixty to ten. The case of Hungary would stand forever as one of the blackest records in Soviet Union history since the Bolshevik Revolution of 1917.

The Middle East and Egypt

The cold war struggle continued to agitate the Middle East during 1957 and early 1958. Specifically, Russian propaganda invented an aggressive war of Turkey against Syria, and, behind the scenes, supported Egypt in bitter denunciation of King Hussein's pro-Western regime in Jordan. The rich oil resources and the strategic position astride the three continents were the stakes.

Following the launching of Sputnik I, the Soviet propaganda machine, working double time, hatched a plot against Turkey. That nation, at the instigation of the United States (so ran the propaganda), was about to attack Syria. The brazen character of that Moscow "big lie" was exposed by Lodge in a major United Nations speech on October 22. Said Lodge, in reply to Soviet Foreign Minister Andrei Gromyko:

Here is a government which has been condemned by the UN three times in the past year for its actions in Hungary . . . accusing the overwhelming majority of the human race of wanting war. . . . Here is the

[5] For Lodge's speech, see p36-46.

chronic lawbreaker, not only seeking to be regarded as a good citizen, but actually trying to sit in the judge's seat and sentence the whole law-abiding community to jail. Here is the arsonist, trying his best to start another fire, and demanding the right to lead the fire brigade.

Lodge added a blunt warning:

The United States will not be stopped by threats or by defamation from continuing to offer its understanding and support to those nations of the Middle East which are being threatened by the Soviet Union and whose independence the Soviet Union seeks to destroy. Let there be no question about our capacity to offer this support. We are strong and our allies are strong.

In effect, Russia had established herself firmly in the power vacuum created by the withdrawal of France and Great Britain. On October 27, 1957, a Technical and Economic Agreement between Syria and Russia was signed in Damascus that "mortgaged Syria's whole future to Russia." The financial aid, "with no strings attached," extended for seven years, and might reach $500 million for dams, irrigation, oil development. The Soviet Union thus came into control of the region that Russia had historically coveted, and now outflanked Turkey and dominated the land to the Persian Gulf. On the heels of the Damascus settlement, the Nasser government of Egypt announced a $175 million loan from Russia for building docks and for industrial development. Nasser had allegedly spurned Western aid "with strings."

In late January 1958 the proposed union of Egypt and Syria was announced; the new "United Arab Republic" was to have one government, one parliament, and one army. Nasser and Cairo were to be in charge. Thus the consolidated nation (joined by Yemen in March), with ample Soviet cooperation, would over-awe and might gradually infiltrate Jordan, Lebanon, Iraq, and even Saudi Arabia.

American debaters, especially Democrats, attacked Dulles repeatedly for his "ineptitude" in his Egyptian and Middle East politics. Why, it was asked, did the United States stand by while Russia established vast power in that strategic region?

Red China

The period of 1957-1958 was one of increasing domestic demand for recognition of the Mao Tse-tung regime. Britain and Japan had expressed their desire to increase their trade with mainland China. From Britain came renewed pressure for the United States to give the nod for the admission of Red China to the United Nations.

Two thirds of the world, it was argued, was either neutral or pro-Communist. Would not America do well to move toward reconciliation with that Far Eastern power with its population of 600 million? Red China, it was argued, would presently dominate the Orient economically and politically; Peiping would no doubt cast off its subserviency to Moscow; and its role in the United Nations would hardly upset the balance more than had already been done by the numerous Soviet vetoes in the Security Council. Formosa, it was argued, could be established as an independent island under the aegis of the United Nations.[6]

DOMESTIC ISSUES

Business and Industry

For the first time since 1944-1945, the issue of inflation and deflation came to the front. In the early months of 1957 the Administration, business leaders, economists, and consumers were more and more concerned with the upward movement of the business cycle. The cost of living index by September was 121.1 as compared with the 1947-1948 average, "the thirteenth consecutive monthly rise." The Federal Reserve Bank continued to step up its discount rates to member banks. Speakers denounced United States Steel for its rise in prices, and unions for their persistent and successful demands for higher wages. Wages and prices, so it was argued, moved in an unbroken chain of inflationary acceleration. More radical critics called for wartime controls and repeated the World War II arguments against national economic destruction through inflation.

[6] For John Foster Dulles' speech, "Our Policies Toward Communism in China," see p47-57.

In September an abrupt change came in the cycle and in the arguments. Steel, automobiles, and other basic production sharply declined. The stock market lost billions in market values. By March 1958 the number of unemployed had reached 5.2 million. The Sputniks and generally oversold markets were partly the cause of the slump. Back and forth swung the market at its lower level. Federal Reserve discount rates were liberalized; Congress lifted the debt ceiling and prepared to vote more than forty billions for national defense; all other government-sponsored projects were set in motion through congressional legislation or Administrative edicts.

The general problem of financing our costly local, state, and Federal governments and of keeping industry at a high level continued in 1958 to furnish no small amount of public eloquence, political and other, and of much more private but universal talk.

Labor

American labor since the amalgamation of the AFL-CIO in 1955 had been receiving a secondary place in national headlines. Few major strikes threatened prolonged economic disturbance. Agitation for repeal of the Taft-Hartley law seemed to have subsided.

When, however, the Senate Committee on Improper Activities in the Labor or Management Field, with Senator John McClellan of Arkansas as chairman, began its investigations in 1957, the issue of labor's status challenged national interest and stimulated debate. Evidence was produced allegedly to prove the widespread use of union funds for the leaders' profits, questionable dealings with management, association between labor leaders and racketeers. These disclosures led to the retirement of Dave Beck, president of the International Brotherhood of Teamsters, and his further indictment and conviction (since appealed) for grand larceny. His successor as president, James R. Hoffa, was also linked with these unsavory associations and practices and also came under indictment.

Early in December 1957 the AFL-CIO expelled the International Brotherhood of Teamsters, and reiterated its determination to carry out its "ethical code." George Meany, president of the AFL-CIO, Walter Reuther, of the United Automobile Workers of America, James B. Carey, of the International Union of Electrical Workers, and other union leaders spoke firmly in support of such a code.[7]

The issue of what legislation, if any, should further curb union activities faced the 1958 Congress and continued to be a subject of discussion throughout the nation. "Right-to-work" laws, already adopted in eighteen states, were further agitated as were other antilabor measures. Meantime, Walter Reuther, in a speech before a convention of the United Automobile Workers, in Detroit on January 23, 1958, proposed that the automobile industry share its profits with the unionists. Negotiations for a new contract with the "Big Three"—Chrysler, Ford, and General Motors—were scheduled to begin in April 1958.

Civil Rights

The prolonged Senate deliberations during July 1957 on civil rights legislation produced one of the most brilliant series of debates in the history of that body during the twentieth century. Far from a highly emotional and prejudicial succession of sectional denunciations, the argument developed as a sound analysis of the constitutional foundations of the American government. The issues were: What civil rights were to be protected? How should they be protected? Should violations of civil rights be tried as contempt citations and decided by Federal judges without juries?

The primary question became one of whether jury trials should be provided for officials cited for contempt of court in cases involving voting rights. Thus the right of trial by jury became central in the debate. Senators Paul Douglas, Samuel Ervin, Jr., Jacob Javits, and Richard Russell, were among the leaders in this month of intense argument.[8] Despite the restrictions in the bill as finally passed, it was held to advance the protection of Negroes' right to vote.

[7] For Carey's speech, "Enemies Within the House of Labor," see p97-110.
[8] See speeches by Douglas, Samuel Ervin, and Wayne Morse, p 111-27.

The Little Rock Case

A more dramatic problem of civil rights arose in the Little Rock, Arkansas, case. Governor Orval Faubus of that state intervened on September 3, 1957, by sending the state guard to prevent nine Negro students from attending the Little Rock high school.

With the continued failure of Governor Faubus to cooperate with the Federal court order to desegregate, and with the gathering of a Little Rock mob that defied the President's proclamation, President Eisenhower ordered one thousand members of the 101st Airborne Division to move into Little Rock for the protection of the Negroes in the school. Eisenhower addressed the nation on the proposition that Federal court orders must be upheld.[9] His position was historically sound—his clear duty was to uphold the Federal court orders.

Governor Faubus took to the air repeatedly in defense of his own position on this special Little Rock case. A large segment of the South denounced the President's order. And the movement toward desegregation was apparently retarded by the use of Federal troops to enforce integration in the Arkansas school.

Education

The Soviet missiles in orbit, just as they stirred public support for national defense, called for the improvement of American education. Where, the public asked, are the future scientists and technicians to come from? Apparently the schools and colleges were not doing their job. And what of the general curriculum? Was it not geared to "life adjustment" rather than to subject matter? Further, how could the schools provide the buildings, equipment, and teachers adequate to handle the increased influx of pupils? And how could the colleges and universities grapple successfully with the increasing tide?

Probably more than any other subject, the topics the American public, lay and professional, talked about were the recognition and encouragement of bright students, scholarships, financing new

[9] For Eisenhower's speech, see p 129-34.

schools, standards of efficiency in teaching, training an adequate supply of teachers and raising current salaries, and budgeting for such expanded programs.[10]

Religion

In 1957 Billy Graham was the outstanding evangelistic preacher of the year, with his historic New York City crusade. His platform fervor and sincerity were unquestioned. His doctrines were orthodox. But his publicity and campaign promotion methods were most modern. As noted in the introduction to the 1956-1957 anthology, "Liberalism, with its interest in the social gospel and the establishment of the Kingdom of God here and now, continued in strong constituency. Theological conservatism and neo-orthodoxy, indicting the trend toward glorifying man rather than God and neglecting historic theology, had their powerful voices." Important spokesmen for the period were Eugene Carson Blake, George A. Buttrick, Edward L. R. Elson, Louis Hadley Evans, Theodore P. Ferris, Harry Emerson Fosdick, Robert Ignatius Gannon, Gerald Hamilton Kennedy, Robert James McCracken, Norman Vincent Peale, Charles E. Shulman, Abba Hillel Silver, Fulton J. Sheen, Samuel Moore Shoemaker, Ralph W. Sockman, and Paul J. Tillich.

[10] For discussions of aspects of the educational problem, see the speeches by G. Keith Funston, "Memo to the Class of 1957," p 135-44; J. Robert Oppenheimer, "Talk to Undergraduates," p 145-56; and J. William Fulbright, "Current Crisis and Need for Education," p 157-61.

SPACE WAR AND NATIONAL DEFENSE

SCIENCE AND NATIONAL SECURITY [1]

DWIGHT D. EISENHOWER [2]

President Dwight D. Eisenhower gave this address to the nation from the White House, on Thursday evening, November 7, 1957. His speech was delivered in the wake of the launching of Russia's Sputnik I, on October 4, and Sputnik II, during the first week of November. The address, labeled in advance as "very important," was broadcast over the radio and television networks and was aimed at a world-wide audience.

The President's speech had four major purposes: (1) to reassure the critics that though the Soviet Union was first with satellites into space, the United States had also made most impressive technological strides; (2) to assure the allies that we would cooperate with them fully in the immediate and later development of military weapons, including intercontinental missiles; (3) to meet the criticism that our alleged missile lag was caused by general administrative and interservice competition and confusion; and (4) to provide evidence that we were abreast of Russia in solving the problem of the long-range ballistic missile.

As President Eisenhower addressed the world, the Soviet Union and its captive countries were celebrating the fortieth anniversary of the Bolshevik Revolution. In the Moscow parades were weapons showing tactical atomic capability. This Soviet celebration glorified the military might of the Soviets.

The President's speech was essentially one of refutation. The speaker, for example, cited thirty-eight types of missiles "either in operation or under construction." He cited in detail the scientific changes and technological advances made by the Army, Navy, and Air Force in their defensive and offensive weapons. He resorted to visual aids in exhibiting to the TV viewers an object that had been fired several hundred miles into space and had been recovered intact. Our scientists, he said, have solved the problem of bringing back a missile from outer space without its burning like a meteor. The entire speech was to contend that the over-all strength of the free world was distinctly greater than that of the Communist countries.

The criticism that administrative confusion and diffusion were responsible for our lag the President met by announcing that he had

---

[1] Text supplied by the White House. For text see also the New York *Times*, November 8, 1957, p 10.

[2] For biographical note, see Appendix.

appointed President James Rhyne Killian, Jr., of the Massachusetts Institute of Technology, to the office of Special Assistant to the President for Science and Technology, to coordinate and integrate missile and rocket production. The Defense Department was to give top priority to missile and rocket development "without regard to interservice rivalries."

Other critics questioned the President's key claim that the "B-52 jet bomber, supported by its jet tankers is standard in our Strategic Air Command." A survey conducted by Edward W. O'Brien, of the Washington Bureau of the St. Louis *Globe Democrat* (November 10, 1957), reported that SAC possessed about 100 B-52's—most of them abroad, in place of the 603 originally designated as necessary—"six times the present fleet." The survey also pointed out that "we have only a handful of KC-135's, the jet counterpart of the B-52. The B-58, to replace the B-52, is not yet in production and military men say that the B-58 never was intended as a replacement for the long range B-52."

The entire speech was a highly personal attempt by the President to vindicate his leadership as a sound military leader in this intercontinental missile and earth satellite age. Immediately after its delivery, the skeptics noted the lack of full responsibility delegated to Dr. Killian. Senator Henry M. Jackson (Democrat, Washington), for example, Chairman of the Atomic Weapons Subcommittee, said that the President had been "less than frank" in describing the state of our defenses, and declared that "we still need a full-time boss for the missiles program at the presidential level." The immediate impression that Killian was to be that "czar" was soon dissipated as his role continued to be vaguely defined.

On Friday, December 6, the Defense Department, to speed up its answer to the Sputniks, attempted to launch the Vanguard, a four-pound test satellite, from the missile test center at Cape Canaveral, Florida. Great publicity attended the event. The rocket, however, exploded on its stand. The failure of this experiment was generally interpreted as a humiliating blow to America's prestige. Senate Majority Leader Lyndon Johnson of Texas asked, "Why don't they perfect the satellite and announce it after it is in the sky?"

On January 31, 1958, came the projection into orbit of the first American satellite, the Army's Explorer, to restore America's prestige around the globe and to counteract the psychological advantage that the Soviets had enjoyed for the two months since Sputnik I began its rotation around the earth. Two other American satellites were launched successfully soon afterward—a Vanguard on March 17 and another Explorer on March 26.

My Fellow Citizens:

My subject tonight is Science in National Security.

Originally this talk was to be part of one I intend to make in Oklahoma City next week. However, I found that I could not possibly deal with this subject in just one address. So tonight I shall concentrate on the most immediate aspects of this question of the relationship of science to the defenses of our country.

First, let me tell you plainly what I am going to do in this talk and in my next.

I am going to lay the facts before you—the rough with the smooth. Some of these security facts are reassuring; others are not—they are sternly demanding. Some require that we resolutely continue lines of action now well begun. Others require new action, and still others new dimensions of effort. After putting these facts and requirements before you, I shall propose a program of action—a program that will demand the energetic support of not just the government but every American, if we are to make it successful.

First, then: some facts about our present security posture. It is one of great strength—but by no means should this assurance satisfy any of us. Our defenses must be adequate not just today, but tomorrow and in all the years to come, until under the safety of these defenses, we shall have secured a durable and just peace for all the world.

As of now, the United States is strong. Our nation has today, and has had for some years, enough power in its strategic retaliatory forces to bring near annihilation to the war-making capabilities of any country.

This position of present strength did not come about by accident. The Korean war had the effect of greatly expanding our peacetime defense forces. As we began the partial demobilization of those forces we undertook also an accelerated program of modernization.

As a first step, scientific surveys were instituted soon after the Korean armistice. The result was a decision to give a "new look" to the defense establishment, depending for increased efficiency more upon modern science and less upon mere numbers of men.

In succeeding years there has been an across-the-board program to bring all units of our defense into line with the possibilities of modern technology. There has been, also, a high level of expenditure on research and development for defense—now running in the aggregate at something over $5 billion a year.

Other scientific surveys following the first one focused attention and emphasis on long-range ballistic missiles. Development on these particular missiles got into high gear more than two years ago. We have since been spending a billion dollars a year on this item alone.

Now, before discussing some of the things we urgently need to do, I would like to give you a few samples of the things that have been done in recent years by our military forces, scientists and engineers to put current scientific discovery at the service of your defense.

In our diversified family of missiles, we have weapons adapted to every kind of distance, launching and use. There are now thirty-eight different types either in operation or under development. And almost one third of these are in actual operation.

All combat vessels of the Navy built since 1955 have guided missiles in place of, or to supplement, guns. The Navy has in both oceans, submarines which can rise to the surface and launch, in a matter of minutes, a missile carrying a nuclear warhead, and submerge immediately—while the missile itself is guided to a target hundreds of miles away.

The Navy possesses atomic depth bombs.

Since Korea, both the Army's and Navy's anti-aircraft guns have been largely replaced by surface-to-air missiles. All of our new interceptor aircraft are armed with air-to-air missiles.

Many of the traditional functions of the Army's artillery and support aircraft have been taken over by guided missiles. For example, we have already produced, in various distance ranges, hundreds of Matador, Honest John and Corporal missiles. To give you some idea of what this means in terms of explosive power: Four battalions of Corporal missiles alone are equivalent in fire power to all the artillery used in World War II on all fronts.

Some of these missiles have their own built-in mechanisms for seeking out and destroying a target many miles away. Thus, the other day, a Bomarc missile, by itself, sought out a fast-moving, unmanned airplane forty-five miles at sea and actually met it head-on.

Except for a dwindling number of B-36's, there is hardly an airplane in the combat units of the Air Force that was in them even as late as the Korean war. The B-52 jet bomber, supported by its jet tankers, is standard in our Strategic Air Command. Again, to show you what this means in terms of power: One B-52 can carry as much destructive capacity as was delivered by all the bombers in all the years of World War II combined. But the B-52 will, in turn, be succeeded by the B-58, a supersonic bomber.

Atomic submarines have been developed. One ran almost sixteen days, recently, without surfacing; another cruised under the polar ice cap for five days.

A number of huge naval carriers are in operation, supplied with the most powerful nuclear weapons and bombers of great range to deliver them. Construction has started which will produce a carrier to be driven by atomic power.

Since 1956 we have developed nuclear explosives with radio-active fall-out of less than 4 per cent of the fallout of previously built weapons. This has obvious importance in developing nuclear defenses for use over our own territory.

In numbers, our stock of nuclear weapons is so large and so rapidly growing that we have been able safely to disperse it to positions assuring its instant availability against attack, and still keep strong reserves. Our scientists assure me that we are well ahead of the Soviets in the nuclear field, both in quantity and in quality. We intend to stay ahead.

We have already shown that we can, with the precision to make it a useful military weapon, fire a large ballistic missile well over a thousand miles. Ballistic test missiles have had successful flights to as much as 3,500 miles. An intercontinental missile is required, and we have some of them in an advanced state of development. But, because of our many forward positions, some of them in the lands of our allies, an intermediate range missile is as good for us as an intercontinental one.

A different kind of missile, the air-breathing Snark, recently traveled over a guided course for 5,000 miles and was accurately placed on target.

We have fired three rockets to heights between 2,000 and 4,000 miles, and have received back much valuable information about outer space.

One difficult obstacle on the way to producing a useful long-range weapon is that of bringing a missile back from outer space without its burning up like a meteor, because of friction with the earth's atmosphere.

Our scientists and engineers have solved that problem. This object here in my office is the nose cone of an experimental missile—fired over a long distance. It has been hundreds of miles into outer space and back. Here it is, completely unharmed—intact.

These illustrations—which are of course only a small sample of our scientists' accomplishments—I give you merely to show that our strength is not static but is constantly moving forward with technological improvement.

Long-range ballistic missiles, as they exist today, do not cancel the destructive and deterrent power of our Strategic Air Force.

The Soviet launching of earth satellites is an achievement of the first importance, and the scientists who brought it about deserve full credit and recognition. Already, useful new facts on outer space have been produced, and more are on the way, as new satellites with added instruments are launched.

Earth satellites, in themselves, have no direct present effect upon the nation's security. However, there is real military significance to these launchings, as I have previously mentioned publicly. Their current military significance lies in the advanced techniques and the competence in military technology they imply; for example, the powerful propulsion equipment necessarily used.

But in the main, the Soviets continue to concentrate on the development of war-making weapons and supporting industries. This, as well as their political attitude in all international affairs, serves to warn us that Soviet expansionist aims have not changed. The world has not forgotten the Soviet military invasions of such countries as Finland and Poland, their support of the war in Korea, or their use of force in their ruthless suppression of Hungarian freedom.

Eternal vigilance and increased free world military power, backed by our combined economic and spiritual strength, provide the only answer to these threats until the Soviet leaders themselves cease to consume their resources in military and expansionist purposes and turn them to the well-being of their own peoples.

We frankly recognize that the Soviets are building up types of power that could, if we were attacked, damage us seriously. This is because no defensive system today can possibly be airtight in preventing all break-throughs of planes and weapons.

To aid in protecting against this, we, in partnership with Canada, have long been constructing a continental defense system reaching from far out in the Pacific, around the northern edge of this continent and across the Atlantic approaches. This is a complex system of early warning radars, communication lines, electronic computers, supersonic aircraft, and ground-to-air missiles, some with atomic warheads. This organization and equipment is under constant improvement; emphasis on this improvement must be increased.

Now, in addition to retaliatory and continental defense forces, we and our allies maintain strong ground and naval units in strategic areas of the world. In the strength and readiness of all these various kinds of power—retaliatory, defensive and local—properly distributed and supported, lies the real deterrent to the outbreak of war. This fact brings home to all of us the tremendous importance to this country of our allies. Not only do they maintain large military forces as part of our combined security, but they provide vital bases and areas that permit the effective deployment of all our forces for defense.

It is my conviction, supported by trusted scientific and military advisers, that, although the Soviets are quite likely ahead in some missile and special areas, and are obviously ahead of us in satellite development, as of today the over-all military strength of the free world is distinctly greater than that of the Communist countries.

We must see to it that whatever advantages they have, are temporary only.

II

Now the next question is: How about the future?

I must say to you, in all gravity, that in spite of both the present over-all strength and the forward momentum of our defense, it is entirely possible that in the years ahead we could fall behind. I repeat: we could fall behind—unless we now face up to certain pressing requirements and set out to meet them promptly.

I address myself now to this problem knowing that for every American it surmounts any divisive influence among us of whatever kind. It reminds us once again that when our security is involved we are not partisans of any kind, we are Americans! We will close ranks as Americans, and get on with the job to be done.

According to my scientific friends, one of our greatest, and most glaring, deficiencies is the failure of us in this country to give high enough priority to scientific education and to the place of science in our national life.

Of course, these scientists, in making that judgment, properly assume that we shall continue to acquire the most modern weapons in adequate numbers as fast as they are produced; but their conviction does expose one great future danger that no amount of money or resources currently devoted to it can fully meet. Education requires time, incentive and skilled teachers.

They believe that a second critical need is that of giving higher priority, both public and private, to basic research.

As to these long range requirements, I shall have something to say next week.

Tonight I shall discuss two other factors, on which prompt action is possible.

The first is the tragic failure to secure the great benefits that would flow from mutual sharing of appropriate scientific information and effort among friendly countries.

Most great scientific advances of the world have been the product of free international exchange of ideas. There is hardly a nation that has not made some significant contribution to modern science.

There instantly comes to mind the contribution of Britain to jet propulsion, radar, and infra-red rays; Germany to rocketry, x-rays, and sulfa drugs; Italy to wireless telegraphy; France to radioactivity; and Japan to magnetics.

In the free world, we all have a lot to give and a lot to gain in security through the pooling of scientific effort. Why should we deny to our friends information that we are sure the Soviets already have?—information our friends could use toward our common security.

Why, for want of the fullest practicable sharing, should we waste American research funds and talent struggling with technological problems already mastered by our friends?

Here is one way in which, at no cost, we can dramatically and quickly magnify the scientific resources at the disposal of the free world.

The second immediate requirement is that of greater concentration of effort and improved arrangements within the government in the fields of science, technology and missiles—including the continuing requirement for the closest kind of executive-legislative cooperation.

III

As to action: I report the following items to you tonight.

The first thing I have done is to make sure that the very best thought and advice that the scientific community can supply, heretofore provided to me on an informal basis, is now fully organized and formalized so that no gap can occur. The purpose is to make it possible for me, personally, whenever there appears to be any unnecessary delay in our development system, to act promptly and decisively.

To that end, I have created a new office called the office of Special Assistant to the President for Science and Technology. This man, who will be aided by a staff of scientists and a strong advisory group of outstanding experts reporting to him and to me, will have the active responsibility of helping me follow through on the program of scientific improvement of our defenses.

I am glad to be able to tell you that this position has been accepted by Dr. James R. Killian, President of the Massachusetts

Institute of Technology. He is a man who holds my confidence, and enjoys the confidence of his colleagues in the scentific and engineering world, and in the government.

Through him, I intend to be assured that the entire program is carried forward in closely-integrated fashion. He will help to see that such things as alleged interservice competition or insufficient use of overtime shall not be allowed to create even the suspicion of harm to our scientific and development program. Moreover, Dr. Killian will see to it that those projects which experts judge have the highest potential shall advance with the utmost possible speed. He will make sure that our best talent and the full necessary resources are applied on certain high-priority top-secret items which, for security reasons, I know you will not expect me to enumerate.

In looking to Dr. Killian to discharge these responsibilities, I know that he will draw upon the full abilities of the scientists and engineers of our country. And let me say that our scientists and engineers, in offering their services to the government in this field, have been generous, patriotic and prompt.

Second: In the Defense Department is an official, directly responsible to the Secretary, in charge of missile development. I have directed that the Secretary make certain that the Guided Missile Director is clothed with all the authority that the Secretary himself possesses in this field. Dr. Killian will, of course, work intimately with this official.

Third: The Secretary of Defense and I have agreed that any new missile or related program hereafter originated will, whenever practicable, be put under a single manager and administered without regard to the separate services.

Fourth: There will be laid before the Congress proposed legislation to remove legal barriers to the exchange of appropriate technological information with friendly countries.

Fifth: If the necessary authority is granted, I shall support, along the lines of the agreement reached recently with Prime Minister Macmillan, a Scientific Committee organized within NATO to carry out an enlarged Atlantic effort in research. Similar action in SEATO and comparable organizations will be studied.

These matters will be discussed in my forthcoming bipartisan meeting with the leaders of Congress. They will be requested to consider every feasible step to hasten needed legislative action. I should like to report to you that on both sides of the aisle down in Congress the leaders have accepted my invitation to come with alacrity and with good will.

These, my friends, are the most immediate steps that are under way in scientific areas as they bear upon security.

Even in two talks I cannot, by any means, cover the entire subject of defense, but only selected questions of pressing and current importance. Accordingly, I am not at this time even alluding to a number of key items bearing strongly on our security, such as mutual aid, and civil defense. Likewise I have not dwelt upon the urgent need for greater dispersal in the Strategic Air Command, or for providing all the means that will enable airplanes to take off in the shortest possible time after receipt of warning.

In this whole effort it is important to see that nothing is wasted on nonessentials. Defense today is expensive, and becoming more so. We cannot afford waste.

It misses the whole point to say that we must now increase our expenditures on all kinds of military hardware and defense— as, for example, to heed demands recently made that we restore all personnel cuts made in the armed forces.

Certainly, we need to feel a high sense of urgency. But this does not mean we should mount our charger and try to ride off in all directions at once.

We must clearly identify the exact and critical needs that have to be met. We must then apply our resources at that point as fully as the need demands. This means selectivity in national expenditures of all kinds. We cannot, on an unlimited scale, have both what we must have and what we would like to have.

We can have a sound defense and the sound economy on which it rests—if we set our priorities and stick to them and if each of us is ready to carry his own share of the burden willingly and without complaint.

In conclusion: Although for tonight's purposes I stress the influence of science on defense, I am not forgetting that there is much more to science than its function in strengthening our defense, and much more to our defense than the part played by science. The peaceful contributions of science—to healing, to enriching life, to freeing the spirit—these are the most important products of the conquest of nature's secrets. And as to our security, the spiritual powers of a nation—its underlying religious faith, its self-reliance, its capacity for intelligent sacrifice—these are the most important stones in any defense structure.

Above all, let me say for all to hear: so far as we are concerned, the amassing of military might never has been—and never will be—devoted to any other end than defense and the preservation of a just peace.

What the world needs today even more than a giant leap into outer space, is a giant step toward peace. Time and again we have demonstrated our eagerness to take such a step. As a start in this direction, I urge the Soviets now to align themselves with the practical and workable disarmament proposals, approved yesterday by a large majority in the United Nations.

Never shall we cease to hope and work for the coming of the day when enduring peace will take these military burdens from the backs of men, and when the scientist can give his full attention, not to human destruction, but to human happiness and betterment.

Thank you. Good night.

TIME FOR ACTION [3]

W. STUART SYMINGTON [4]

Senator W. Stuart Symington (Democrat, Missouri), gave this off-the-cuff speech before the Kiwanis Club, at Hannibal, Missouri, on November 4, 1957. It was typical of scores of his talks before Missouri community clubs, and over radio and television from Washington, D.C. during the closing weeks of 1957.

The Senator, formerly Secretary of the Air Force, had urged for the previous ten years a strong national defense, including an air arm sufficient to keep pace with that of Russia. His repeated propositions were that Russia had steadily increased the total attacking force; that the threat to our security was great and that we were relatively falling behind just as did England in 1938-1939; that the American people had not been properly informed about our national defense; and that the national Defense Department had been inefficient and therefore was in urgent need of wholesale reorganization.[5]

Symington, in an address on October 14, 1957, on the significance of the Sputnik in American defense policy, placed the full responsibility for our lag in missile and rocket development squarely on President Eisenhower. He stated: "In some ways, the successful launching of this satellite may be a blessing in disguise, because it tears down once and for all the veil of unreality that some have cast over the relative military strength of the United States and the free world vis-à-vis the military strength of the Soviet Communists and their earth-bound satellites."

Symington's address of November 4 reiterated his vehement declaration—"It is clear that the American people have been misled"—and called for immediate presidential action. Paul Butler, chairman of the Democratic National Committee, stated on November 14: "Senator Symington's knowledgeable warnings during the past five years that we should come into the situation with which we are faced today constitutes a magnificent contribution not for our party but for our country." Butler charged that until very recently the Symington warnings had been "tossed off as so much gobbledygook." [6]

On February 5, 1956, in a *Meet the Press* NBC television interview, Symington said, "I don't *believe* the Soviets are ahead of us in ballistics

[3] Text with permission for this reprint furnished through the courtesy of Senator W. Stuart Symington.

[4] For biographical note, see Appendix.

[5] See for example Symington's earlier addresses in *Representative American Speeches: 1949-50*, p75-84, "Freedom and Military Security; *1952-53*, p42-48, "The Truth Makes Us Free."

[6] St. Louis *Globe-Democrat*, November 15, 1957, p5.

missiles. I state that they *are*. They have fired long-range missiles hundreds of miles further than we have."

Senator Symington's demand for action was decisively fulfilled on January 31, 1958 with the launching of the first Explorer; with the announcement of outer space projects to be under the supervision of Secretary McElroy, of the Defense Department; and with the setting up of an Advanced Research Projects Agency, under General Electric's vice president, Roy W. Johnson.

Senator Symington is a highly competent speaker, free from the "grand manner style" of many political speakers of a former generation. He has facility in speech composition, including extempore utterance, excellent vocal adjustment and articulate clarity in his radio and television presentations, as well as in his talks before community and educational audiences.

The date of the launching of the first satellite, October 4, 1957, is the date of a technological Pearl Harbor for the United States.

It is now clear the people have been misled.

There is no use crying over spilled milk, because the past is the past.

But how about the present—and above all, how about the future?

The people now demand action. Are they getting that action? They are not. Over four weeks have passed since that first launching. What has been done to speed up our defense program? Nothing.

There have been many conferences, and briefings of surprised officials, and we have been promised more speeches. But what the people now demand is more action and less talk.

The launching of the first satellite proved the Soviet Communists had at least the thrust necessary to launch an intermediate range ballistic missile. The launching of the second satellite proves the Soviets now have more thrust than is necessary to launch an intercontinental ballistic missile—and therefore this second launching lends great weight to the Russian announcement some time ago that they had perfected the weapon we fear the most.

Because of the thrust and guidance capacity displayed in these two launchings, only an ignorant man, or somebody worse, will from here out continue to try to persuade the American people that we are ahead of the Communists in the all-important long-range ground-to-ground ballistic missile field. The truth is we are at least two years behind; and, under present policies and programs, can only fall further behind every day.

It is fortunate for ourselves and our allies the Soviets know that as of today, if they dare launch an attack against the United States, SAC, America's Strategic Air Command, can in turn destroy Russia. This deterrent capacity of SAC is the great current deterrent to any all-out war. It has been so for many years.

This capacity cannot be effective for long under present policies, however; because, as Russian defenses against manned aircraft steadily improve, nevertheless the United States, for purely fiscal reasons, has been cutting back and slowing down the modernization of its Strategic Air Force. For purely fiscal reasons, SAC's maintenance and operation funds have been retarded. As a result we have been having more unnecessary accidents. For purely fiscal reasons, we have been retarding the training of both the operation crews, and the maintenance crews upon which so much of the security of our nation depends.

These policies of reduction apply not only to the Strategic Air Force, but also to other Commands of the Air Force, and Commands of the Army, and of the Navy; and not only to the Regulars, but also to the Reserves.

In the face, therefore, of the now visibly growing Russian military might, this Administration first decided upon a policy of unilateral disarmament, and now is in the process of carrying it out.

Not many people realize that, even as of today, in America's long-range Strategic Air Force there are more wings of the relatively ancient piston-driven B-36 than there are of the more modern B-52's. To the best of my knowledge, the B-36 is the oldest combat airplane in either the United States or the Soviet Air Force; it was designed in 1941, before this country entered World War II. Nevertheless the production of B-52's has also been slowed down and cut back.

There is nothing more important to the future security of this country than to have a substantial portion of our Strategic Air Force on the alert at all times. But few people realize that last year much of this Strategic Air Force was grounded because of lack of funds—actually grounded for many weeks at a time.

One thing is sure, however—the Soviets knew it.

It is understood the Congress now plans some hearings on this question of relative defense strength; and that is good, because such hearings should focus attention on the growing peril.

Again, what is important now, however, is the future—not the past.

But military and scientific experts are now saying, "Why all the surprise? In the Airpower Subcommittee hearings of the Senate we told you under oath what was happening—and what would happen if our policies were not radically changed. They were not changed. In fact, the slow-downs and cutbacks and further fiscal limitations were increased—so why the surprise?"

The record of those hearings has been published by the Congress. Why not read them yourself, and make your own decision?

As I write, the morning paper has been brought in. On the front page is a headline—"U. S. Makes No Speed-Up on Missiles—Program Still on 5-Day Week Despite Sputniks."

Speed-up? Most of the Commands of the Army, Navy and Air Force have recently been heavily reduced, in modernization, in personnel, in personnel training, and in funds for adequate maintenance and operations. Nor has there been any acceleration in the tempo of the missile program.

This is unfortunate, because time is of the essence. Time is one asset which, once lost, can never be regained. Yet, over four precious weeks have already been irretrievably lost.

The President should end all the excuses and sweet talk which is now coming out of his Administration and his official family. Conferences are important. Committees are important. Hearings are important. Diplomatic negotiations with our allies are important. But most important is action, because the record proves the Soviets will only laugh at any efforts to establish world peace if those efforts are negotiated by us from a position of relative weakness instead of one of relative strength.

The Congress as well as the people they represent want to know what broad but practical steps are being taken now, in both the military and scientific fields, to meet the growing danger.

Another nation, with a sad and terrible record, has now hitched the wagon of its future to the stars. The truth can no longer be evaded.

Once it was only the words of such great patriots as Bradley and Carney, Killian and Teller, Bedell Smith and Spaatz.

Now the truth is in the sky, for all to see.

Let us have done with the appeasers who say that those who demand action are guilty of hysteria and panic. That kind of talk is too reminiscent for comfort of the days of Stanley Baldwin.

In a period of Britain's growing peril, Winston Churchill spoke of a time when "short-sighted opinions, agreeable to the party spirit, pernicious to national interests, banished all purpose from the state."

Let us hope that those who have put a balanced budget ahead of our national security will ponder well that statement.

Of course we should race the Russians in the long-range missile field. Our future security depends upon the outcome of that race. But the United States will not have an intercontinental ballistic missile in operational quantities for years to come—and therefore our security at this time depends upon the strength of our existing forces, Army, Navy and Air. The plans and programs for these existing forces therefore should be ones of acceleration instead of deceleration.

So let us also hope that the President, in recognizing the scope of the problem, in our diplomacy, in science, in education, as well as in military strength, will present immediately to the Congress a broad and constructive new program.

Four and a half precious weeks have already been lost.

America wants to go to work, so as to be strong in order to remain free.

SOVIET SUPPRESSION OF HUNGARIAN LIBERTY [7]

HENRY CABOT LODGE, JR.[8]

Henry Cabot Lodge, Jr., chief United States delegate to the United Nations, gave this speech before the General Assembly of the United Nations, on September 10, 1957.

The Assembly had been called into special session to consider the adoption of a report submitted by the United Nations committee of five, appointed to investigate the facts concerning the suppression of Hungary.

On October 23, 1956, the Hungarian students and intellectuals, in a Budapest meeting, called for the withdrawal of Soviet troops from Hungary. Twenty-four hours later another meeting was fired upon by the Soviet-dominated military. A general uprising followed throughout the nation. The overwhelming military might and tanks of the Soviets brutally suppressed the "rebels." Within two weeks the revolution was crushed. Thousands were killed. Other thousands managed to flee to the free West. Other thousands were rounded up and shipped to the Soviet slave camps.

The General Assembly, on the heels of this tragedy, adopted resolutions calling on the Soviet occupation forces to withdraw, and on the Soviet regime of Janos Kadar to admit United Nations observers to Hungary. The Soviets ignored this General Assembly request.

In June 1957, the five-member committee completed its report, of some 150,000 words, in which the Soviet Union was charged with ruthless suppression of a "popular uprising."

The General Assembly resolution, sponsored by the United States and thirty-six other nations, called for further condemnation of the Soviets and further demand for them to withdraw from Hungary.

On September 14, 1957, after four days of general debate, with bitter reply from the Soviet representatives, the resolution with some amendments was passed by a vote of sixty to ten, with ten abstentions.

This Hungarian tragedy and the accompanying United Nations debates were merely another chapter in the prolonged Soviet propaganda war.[9]

---

[7] Text furnished by Henry Cabot Lodge, Jr., with permission for this reprint. Because of the length of this United Nations address, only a section is here included.

[8] For biographical note, see Appendix.

[9] For previous records of this warfare, see, for example, Warren Austin, "The Big Lie," *Representative American Speeches: 1950-51*, p 13-24; Henry Cabot Lodge, Jr., "Stop Being Afraid," *1950-51*, p37-43; Henry Cabot Lodge, Jr., "Hungary's Struggle for Freedom," *1956-57*, p36-39.

Ambassador Lodge, as we have remarked in previous editions, has repeatedly met, blow for blow, the Soviet vocal propaganda barrage, with the U.S.S.R.'s vituperation, distortion of facts, and hypocritical posturing as the spokesman for all "anti-capitalistic," "anti-imperialistic," "pro-democratic," "liberty- and peace-loving" races and nations.

Lodge has steadily improved in his persuasive marshaling of facts and constructive sentiments and in voicing the mind of the free world.

Mr. President:

In reconvening its Eleventh Session to consider further the problem of Hungary, the General Assembly is showing once again its high sense of duty. We have to deal with a gross defiance of the United Nations and with deep suffering inflicted on a brave people. No matter what the difficulties or how great the odds may seem, we must do all that we can to uphold the right. If today we are faithful to our trust under the Charter, a peaceful return to justice will surely come to pass in good time. . . . .

The Revolution and Its Suppression

As to the events which the Committee's report recounts, I shall mention only the most significant points. The report proves with detailed, first-hand evidence that what happened in Hungary between October 23 and the middle of November 1956 was a simple struggle by nearly a whole people to regain their lost liberty, a struggle snuffed out by massive Soviet force.

On October 22, 1956, as throughout the previous nine years, Hungry was held captive by the Soviet Union. On the next day the Hungarian people began to march toward freedom. One week later Hungary was free. For a period of four days ending in the early hours of November 4, Hungary had emerged from captivity. During this period the Soviet Union even made a semblance of acknowledging the country's new status and pretended to negotiate with it on withdrawing Soviet troops.

At the same time the Hungarian regime itself was changing. Within the first twenty-four hours of the uprising, it became clear that the old-style Communist police state was without power to maintain itself. The resources of power at its disposal since 1947 turned out to be a mere shadow. The army melted away and the

Moscow-inspired secret police, the AVH, was too deeply hated to be a source of strength.

By contrast, the revolutionary forces, which included all elements of society in Hungary acting in complete unity and driven by the desire for freedom, possessed the power to remove the regime. Theirs was the most violent challenge to Communist despotism ever to erupt in Eastern Europe. In one short week the Hungarian people secured the formation of a government by men of their choice. It was pledged to domestic policies of a socialist nature within a democratic framework; a multiparty system based on free and secret elections; the withdrawal of Soviet troops; and the pursuance of a neutral foreign policy. In this connection let me interject that the United States has never thought that a free Hungary would or should have other than a neutral foreign policy or that it should be brought into any military alliance with the West.

The Hungarian Communist party, with an allegedly reliable membership of nearly 900,000, disappeared overnight. The hated secret police was disbanded, its best-known leaders and members killed or forced into hiding. Statues of Stalin, Soviet memorials and various outward signs of the country's former status as a colony of Moscow were destroyed by aroused multitudes of young and old.

Free political parties, newly reformed or revived, succeeded the imposed single Communist party. A free press was in vigorous operation. Moscow publicly ordered Soviet occupation troops to withdraw from Budapest since their presence "could serve as an excuse for a further aggravation of the situation."

At that moment this spontaneous popular revolt had reached the pinnacle of success. Order was being restored throughout the country when, on November 4, Soviet armies forcibly deposed the popular regime and proceeded to reimpose on the people of Hungary the same system of terror against which they had rebelled.

These are not simply political events with which we are dealing, Mr. President. They are human events, and it is primarily in that human light that I hope we in this General Assembly will view them. The Special Committee clearly saw the human meaning of their assignment. We who have read their report will remember not only its political analysis but, perhaps even more, the words and acts of people like the girl who told the committee what she considered the cause of the October 23 revolution: "We, the young people," she said, "were particularly hampered because we were brought up amidst lies. We continually had to lie. We could not have a healthy idea because everything was choked in us. We wanted freedom of thought."

Hungary Since November—The Promise and the Betrayal

It remains now to review some of the events since Moscow reimposed its rule on Hungary by the military attack of November 4. In the opinion of the United States this part of the story is of crucial importance. We must consider it with close attention if we are to do justice to the human problem which confronts us. . . .

Promise Number One: Withdrawal of Soviet troops.

The November 4 program of the puppet regime stated in point 15:

"After the restoration of calm and order the Hungarian government will begin negotiations with the Soviet government and with the other participants to the Warsaw Pact on the withdrawal of Soviet troops from Hungary." Mr. Kadar repeated this promise on the radio and to visiting delegations on November 8, November 11, November 14, November 15, and November 28. His foreign minister, Mr. Horvath, repeated it here in the General Assembly on December 3, 1956, in these words: "As soon as order is restored, Janos Kadar will demand the withdrawal of Soviet troops from Hungary."

Mr. President, that promise has been broken. A conservative estimate made by the United States Government places the present number of Soviet troops in Hungary, not counting air force contingents, at 68,000, compared to only 25,000 in September 1956, before the revolution.

The very notion of negotiations to remove these troops was officially abandoned as early as May 11 when Mr. Kadar said to the National Assembly in Budapest: "We are supporters of the Warsaw Treaty and consequently we are also supporters of the presence of Soviet troops in Hungary, as long as we are faced with the aggressive ambitions of the imperialists and the gathering of the imperialists' forces." Translated out of Communist jargon, Mr. President, that amounts to indefinite postponement.

Promise Number Two: No reprisals against Freedom Fighters.

The newly installed regime promised on November 4: "The government will not tolerate the persecution of workers under any pretext for having taken part in the most recent events." Again on November 26 in a radio broadcast Mr. Kadar said: "I repeatedly and unequivocally declare that we will adhere to, and make every one adhere to, the solemn promise made in our government's appeal of November 4, that no worker will come to harm as a result of his participation in the mass movement which began on October 23."

It is hard to see why this promise had to be limited to workers, since in most societies justice is accorded impartially to all people regardless of their occupation or their supposed membership in one or another social class. But even if we let that pass, the record shows that the authorities in Hungary have broken their solemn promise of no reprisals, and have gone back to the old system of police terror.

We have a news report that all three hundred workers in a factory in Miskolc, one of the strongholds of the revolution, were sent to Russia for a "study visit" and have not been heard from since. We have reports of new networks of informers being created in factories and villages by blackmail threats against people who took part in the uprising. As usual in a police state, some of these reports cannot be fully verified.

But on April 20, the provincial paper *Zalai Hirlap,* in western Hungary, officially revealed the indictment of the whole population of the town of Lenti, whose population in 1944 was 2,370, for taking part in the revolution—the whole town.

In further proof of the breaking of this promise, Mr. President, the United States Delegation has submitted, for circulation as a General Assembly document, a list of 1,768 individuals, each identified by name, against whom the Hungarian authorities have taken punitive action between November 1956 and August 1957 for alleged anti-regime activities during and after the October revolution. This list is drawn entirely from Hungarian Communist sources, namely Hungarian newspapers and Hungarian Communist radio broadcasts during the period in question. This is the nearest thing to official information available in Hungary today. The list is doubtless incomplete but it is the best we have been able to get.

It shows 23 executions.

It shows 51 death sentences.

It shows 29 sentences of life imprisonment, 15 of them commuted from sentences of death.

Among the occupations listed are: worker in a wagon factory; coach builder; delivery man; apprentice; waiter; truck driver; foreman; driver; cabinet maker; miner; electrician. Even by Communist standards I think such people are called workers. Other listed occupations, no less honorable, are student; bank clerk; soldier; army officer; university professor; writer; musician.

Of all these charges, the most frequent is the simple phrase "revolutionary activity."

Many of those listed were reported simply as arrested. That is the last word we have about them. Perhaps the Hungarian authorities or the Soviet government can tell us what happened to them.

Because of the breaking of this promise, Mr. President, not only these 1,768 people have been hurt, together with all others persecuted whose names have not been published. The entire Hungarian people are hurt when the courts are used in this way to make examples and thus to frighten the people into obedience.

This list, of course, does not include any individuals against whom proceedings have been taken but not reported in the newspapers. We have no way of knowing accurately how many of these there may be, although some reports indicate the number is in the tens of thousands. Nor does it include the 190,000

Hungarians who fled to other countries rather than risk the vengeance of the Soviet puppet regime. They too, I might say, have been receiving letters full of promises of good treatment if they return to Hungary, but they know well enough how much faith to put in such promises.

Promise Number Three: A multiparty system.

On November 4 Mr. Kadar said in a radio broadcast that certain portfolios in his cabinet "must be filled by representatives of other parties and nonparty persons." On November 11 he said again in a radio seech: "I can't imagine the solution of our future tasks otherwise than by responsible participation of men of different party-political and ideological views in the country's government at all levels."

This promise too was broken. By November 26 Mr. Kadar was saying on the radio that it would be fulfilled "once productive work has started throughout the country and legal order has been restored everywhere in every aspect." That is quite a condition, and evidently it has not yet been fulfilled. On May 27 of this year the Minister of the Interior, Mr. Biszku, said in a public lecture that the efforts to restore other parties were "reactionary." That is the old word. He said "In our country the multiparty system doesn't serve the interests of the dictatorship of the proletariat, it would only give the reaction legal possibilities." So much for the right of political opposition.

Promise Number Four: Free elections.

Point 11 in the November 4 program of the Kadar regime was "the securing of democratic elections." Again on November 15 he told a delegation from the Greater Budapest Workers' Council: "We surrender the Party's monopoly: We want a multiparty system and clean and honest elections. We know that this will not be easy, because the workers' power can be destroyed not only by bullets but also by ballots. We must reckon with the fact that we might be thoroughly beaten at the elections, but we undertake the election fight because the Communist Party will have the strength to gain once more the confidence of the working masses."

That was a categorical promise made by a man with his eyes open. It was of the utmost political importance. It has been broken. On May 9 Mr. Kadar told the National Assembly "The Government takes the view that in our present position it would not be correct if we expended our time and strength on parliamentary elections." The National Assembly thereupon passed a constitutional amendment prolonging its own mandate and postponing elections for two years. Whether the elections will be held after two years, and if so whether they will give the people the kind of real choice Mr. Kadar spoke of on November 15 is impossible to tell. But the signs are far from encouraging.

Promise Number Five: The right to strike.

On December 11, 1956, the National Association of Free Hungarian Trade Unions, which was a government-sponsored organization and can be presumed to speak for the regime, declared: "The right to strike is the inalienable right of the workers' class." And again: "The strike is the strong weapon of the workers' class."

The promise clearly implied in that statement was broken. Decrees No. 2 and No. 4 of 1957, by the Presidential Council, established the death penalty for inciting to strike or advocating a strike in any shop with more than one hundred workers.

Promise Number Six: An end to the Soviet plunder of Hungary.

On November 14, 1956, Mr. Kadar told representatives of several workers' councils that in future all trade agreements entered into by Hungary would be made public. The next day his statement was confirmed in a state radio broadcast.

This promise held special importance for the Hungarian people because one of the motives behind the uprising was to get rid of suspected economic exploitation of Hungary by the Soviet Union, especially in the uranium mines. Yet this promise too was broken. On June 16, 1957, Decree 34 classified as state secrets all data about trade negotiations and trade relations and agreements between Hungary and foreign countries.

Promise Number Seven: Freedom for writers and artists.

On January 6, 1957, Radio Budapest broadcast a government declaration which said: "The Government insures freedom for scientific and artistic creative work and respect for scientific and artistic convictions. Every progressive tendency and conception which promotes the development of our national culture must be given room in scientific and artistic life."

This promise, ambiguous enough to begin with, was soon broken completely by the institution of police terror against Hungarian writers. On January 17 the Hungarian Writers' Union was temporarily suspended by the police. On January 25 Radio Budapest announced the arrest of five prominent writers for revolutionary activity. On April 21 the Writers' Union was permanently abolished and the famous writer Tibor Dery was arrested, according to Radio Budapest, "on suspicion of having committed a crime against the State." We have no word that Mr. Dery has yet been released. These arrests, undoubtedly, have helped to make sure that the only freedom exercised by Hungarian writers is the freedom to write as they are told, or not write at all.

Promise Number Eight: Freedom of religion.

On November 27 the State Office for Church Affairs, a part of the government, said: "The Revolutionary Worker-Peasant Government stands on the basis of free practice of religion." Specifically the announcement confirmed the privilege of religious instruction in schools, which was one demand of the revolution.

This promise too was broken. On January 29 a decree was issued permitting attendance at religious classes only for children who had been enrolled for them at the beginning of the school year. Since the beginning of the school year was before the revolution when restrictions on this matter were still in force, the new decree took away with one hand what had been given with the other. It was a transparent piece of evasion.

Mr. President, there are eight broken promises of the regime in Hungary. The list could be extended. But I have chosen these eight because they all concern basic rights of every human being. Judged by the standards which it set for itself, the Soviet puppet regime has grievously wronged the Hungarian people.

That regime is, of course, an agent of Moscow's will. The wrongs it has done flow from the original wrong done by Moscow in crushing Hungary's liberty and independence by armed force. . . . .

Mr. President, this is an important decision to make and, I suggest, essential to progress. The people of Hungary are being shot and imprisoned and maltreated now; their sufferings are actual and acute and demand from one day to the next to be relieved. It is impossible to know how many lives of Hungarian patriots are endangered from one day to the next day by continuation of the present grim course of events in that country. If we are to come to the relief of these people we must at least begin to do so with all speed. That means that we must not let this matter drift but keep it in the forefront of our attention until we know that progress is being made.

Conclusion

Mr. President, the greatest danger which we face in this difficult and tragic matter is that we will give in to despair. The most necessary quality for us, therefore, is steadfastness. We know what is right. Although there is considerable physical power behind the thing which is wrong, those who wield that power are human beings who can be brought to change their minds. It is not only in our interest, but in theirs as well, that that change should occur. Until it does they will continue to be surrounded, as they are today, by bitter and hostile peoples who will turn against them the minute they have the chance.

In a speech last May 9 to the National Assembly in Budapest, Mr. Kadar is reported to have rejected proposed political reforms in his Soviet-occupied state by saying "we cannot turn back the wheel of history." Mr. President, I think there is great doubt that Mr. Kadar and his Soviet masters know in which direction the wheel of history is turning. They seem to be trying with all their might to wrench it out of its natural path. But surely it cannot forever be made to turn in a direction which causes so much death and fear and heartache and suffering for millions of people. The faith of the sponsors of this resolution is that the wheel of history can, with God's help and steadfast human effort, be made to move toward justice and toward truth.

OUR POLICIES TOWARD COMMUNISM IN CHINA [10]

JOHN FOSTER DULLES [11]

The Honorable John Foster Dulles, Secretary of State, gave this address at the Convention of the Lions International, at San Francisco, California, on June 28, 1957.

The audience of several thousand roundly applauded the speaker as he reiterated the determination of the United States to continue its opposition to the recognition of the Communist Chinese Peiping Government.

Secretary Dulles, in this major foreign policy pronouncement (as he announced it), the first comprehensive statement in three years by the State Department on this issue, averred that Chinese communism was a "passing, and not a perpetual phase," and was not to be supported by our recognition. He opposed economic, diplomatic, commercial, or political aid to Red China.

The speech was delivered in a period of increasing domestic demand for such recognition of the Mao Tse-tung regime. Britain and Japan had recently expressed willingness to increase their trade with mainland China, and had been busy building up pressure on this country for the admission of that nation to the United Nations.

Although the speaker did not mention the current issue related to the State Department's ban on United States reporters visiting Red China, he commented that "we doubt the value of cultural exchanges which the Chinese Communists are eager to develop."

Dulles set forth with full details four main arguments against such recognition. Chief among his conclusions was that China's entry into the United Nations would make her a "veto-wielding member of the Security Council." The result might be to implant in the United Nations the "seeds of destruction" of that organization.

Cogent as was Dulles' case, changing events later in 1957 suggested strong criticism of his stand. It was widely pointed out that two thirds of the world was either neutral or pro-Communist, and that America would do well diplomatically to move toward reconciliation with the Far East power with its six hundred millions. It was argued that whether we like it or not, China would presently develop huge economic and political leadership in the Orient; that its communism was not cut to the line of Marxism and that its independence of Moscow was more and more apparent; that an additional Communist veto in the Security Council would

[10] Text supplied by the Public Service Division of the Department of State, with permission for this reprint through the courtesy of the Secretary of State John Foster Dulles.

[11] For biographical note, see Appendix.

hardly change the pattern there since the Russian veto itself, often applied, had repeatedly registered the position of the official Communist world; that to continue withholding recognition was creating a wall around ourselves even more than around China; that when Chiang Kai-shek died his Nationalist regime would also decline; and that Formosa could well be established as an independent nation under the aegis of the United Nations.[12]

It is appropriate that in this great city of San Francisco, which faces the Far East, we should consider our policies toward communism in China.

On the China mainland 600 million people are ruled by the Chinese Communist party. That party came to power by violence and, so far, has lived by violence.

It retains power not by will of the Chinese people but by massive, forcible repression. It fought the United Nations in Korea: it supported the Communist war in Indo-China; it took Tibet by force. It fomented the Communist Huk rebellion in the Philippines and the Communists' insurrection in Malaya. It does not disguise its expansionist ambitions. It is bitterly hateful of the United States, which it considers a principal obstacle in the way of its path of conquest.

In the face of this condition the United States has supported, morally and materially, the free nations of the Western Pacific and Southeast Asia. Our security treaties make clear that the violation of these nations by international communism would be considered as endangering our own peace and safety and that we would act accordingly.

Together we constitute a goodly company and a stout bulwark against aggression.

As regards China, we have abstained from any act to encourage the Communist regime, morally, politically, or materially. Thus:

We have not extended diplomatic recognition to the Chinese Communist regime;

We have opposed its seating in the United Nations;

We have not traded with Communist China or sanctioned cultural interchanges with it.

[12] For comment on Dulles as a speaker, see the Cumulative Author Index for references to his speeches in earlier volumes of *Representative American Speeches*.

These have been, and are, our policies. Like all our policies, they are under periodic review.

As we review our China policy, we naturally and properly recall our recognition policy as regards Communist Russia.

The Bolsheviks seized power from Kerensky in 1917. Nevertheless, we continued for sixteen years to treat the Kerensky representatives in exile as representing the lawful government of Russia. By 1933 it seemed that the Communist regime might be considered as a peaceful member of society. For more than a decade it had committed no act of armed aggression. It had accepted the independence of Estonia, Latvia, and Lithuania, and of Poland. It was not demonstrably maltreating American citizens. It promised to cease subversive activities in the United States, to respect American rights in Russia, and to settle Russia's public and private debts to the United States.

Also, by 1933, we desired to encourage the Soviet regime to resist Japanese aggressive policies in the Far East. The Republic of China, inspired by this same notion, had recognized the Soviet government in December 1932, and we shortly followed suit.

We need not question that act of recognition under the circumstances which then prevailed. Recognition seemed indicated by many tests, and we did not read the future.

However, it can, I think, be said with confidence that recognition would not have been accorded to the Soviet Union even in 1933 had there been clear warning that the Soviet promises given in that connection were totally unreliable, that aggressive war would soon become an instrumentality of Soviet policy, and that it would be neutral toward Japanese aggression in Asia.

In the case of Communist China we are forewarned. That regime fails to pass even those tests which, after sixteen years, the Soviet regime seemed to pass.

Soviet Russia, in 1933, had had a decade of peaceful and non-aggressive relations with neighboring states; Communist China's past record is one of armed aggression.

The Soviet regime seemed to want peace for the future. In the case of Communist China the situation is quite the reverse. Mr. Chou En-lai, at the time of the Bandung conference, said that "the Chinese people do not want to have war with the United States and are willing to settle international disputes by peaceful means." But when the United States took him up and sought explicit reciprocal renunciations of force, his ambassador, after presenting various evasive formulas, finally stated frankly that his regime did intend to use armed force to take Taiwan (Formosa) unless they could get it in some other way.

The Soviet Union in 1933 was not flagrantly violating its international engagements. The Chinese Communist regime is violating the 1953 Korean armistice and the 1954 Indo-China armistice.

There was reason to hope that the Soviet regime would treat our nationals with respect. The Chinese Communist regime violates the persons of our citizens in defiance of the elementary code of international decency and it breaches its 1955 pledge to release them.

It seemed, in 1933, that the Soviet regime and the United States had parallel interests in resisting Japanese aggression in the Far East. Today the political purposes of Communist China clash everywhere with our own.

United States diplomatic recognition of Communist China would have the following consequences:

The many mainland Chinese, who by Mao Tse-tung's own recent admission seek to change the nature of their government, would be immensely discouraged.

The millions of overseas Chinese would feel that they had no Free China to which to look. Today increasing numbers of these overseas Chinese go to Free China to study. Six years ago there were less than one hundred Chinese students from Southeast Asia and Hong Kong studying in Taiwan. Now there are nearly five thousand.

The number of Chinese students from overseas communities coming to Free China has increased year by year; the number going to Communist China has declined, and hundreds of disillusioned students have made their way out of mainland China in the past two years.

If the United States recognized the Chinese Communist regime, many of the millions of overseas Chinese in free Asian countries would, reluctantly, turn to acceptance of the guiding direction of the Communist regime. This would be a tragedy for them; and it would imperil friendly governments already menaced by Chinese Communist subversion.

The Republic of China, now on Taiwan, would feel betrayed by its friend. That government was our ally in the Second World War and for long bore alone the main burden of the Far Eastern war. It had many tempting opportunities to compromise with the Japanese on terms which would have been gravely detrimental to the United States. It never did so. We condemn the Soviets for having dishonored their twenty-year treaty pledge of 1945 to support the Chinese national government as the central government of China. We are honor-bound to give our ally, to whom we are pledged by a mutual defense treaty, a full measure of loyalty.

4. The free Asian governments of the Pacific and Southeast Asia would be gravely perplexed. They are not only close to the vast Chinese land mass, but geographically and, to some extent, politically, they are separated as among themselves. The unifying and fortifying influence is, above all, the spirit and resolution of the United States. If we seemed to waver and to compromise with communism in China, that would in turn weaken free Asia resistance to the Chinese Communist regime and assist international communism to score a great success in its program to encircle us.

United States recognition of Communist China would make it probable that the Communist regime would obtain the seat of China in the United Nations. That would not be in the interest either of the United States or of the United Nations.

The United Nations is not a reformatory for bad governments. It is supposedly an association of those who are already "peace-loving" and who are "able and willing to carry out" the charter obligations. The basic obligation is not to use force, except in defense against armed attack.

The Chinese Communist regime has a record of successive armed aggressions, including war against the United Nations itself, a war not yet politically settled but discontinued by an armistice. The regime asserts not only its right but its purpose to use force if need be to bring Taiwan under its rule.

The Republic of China is entitled to a permanent seat and veto power in the Security Council. Should a regime which in seven years has promoted five foreign or civil wars—Korea, Indo-China, Tibet, the Philippines, and Malaya; which itself has fought the United Nations and which today stands condemned by the United Nations as an aggressor; which defies the United Nations' decision to reunify Korea, and which openly proclaims its continuing purpose to use force—should that regime be given a permanent seat, with veto power, in the body which under the charter has "primary responsibility for the maintenance of international peace and security"?

Communist Russia, with its veto power, already seriously limits the ability of the United Nations to serve its intended purposes. Were Communist China also to become a permanent, veto-wielding member of the Security Council, that would, I fear, implant in the United Nations the seeds of its own destruction.

Let me turn now to the matter of trade and cultural relations, which could exist, to a limited degree, without recognition.

Normal peacetime trade with China, from which the American and Chinese peoples would benefit, could be in the common interest. But it seems that that kind of trade is not to be had in any appreciable volume.

Trade with Communist China is not a normal trade. It does not provide one country with what its people want but cannot well produce for themselves, in exchange for what other people want but cannot well produce for themselves. Trade with Communist China is wholly controlled by an official apparatus, and its limited amounts of foreign exchange are used to develop as rapidly as possible a formidable military establishment and a heavy industry to support it. The primary desire of that regime is for machine tools, electronic equipment, and, in general, what will help it produce tanks, trucks, planes, ammunition, and such military items.

Whatever others may do, surely the United States, which has heavy security commitments in the China area, ought not build up the military power of its potential enemy.

We also doubt the value of cultural exchanges, which the Chinese Communists are eager to develop. They want this relationship with the United States primarily because, once that example were given, it would be difficult for China's close neighbors not to follow it. These free nations, already exposed to intense Communist subversive activities, could not have the cultural exchanges that the Communists want without adding greatly to their danger.

These are the considerations which argue for a continuance of our present policies. What are the arguments on the other side?

There are some who say that we should accord diplomatic recognition to the Communist regime because it has now been in power so long that it has won the *right* to that.

That is not sound international law. Diplomatic recognition is always a privilege, never a right.

Of course, the United States knows that the Chinese Communist regime exists. We know that very well, for it has fought us in Korea. Also, we admit of dealing with the Chinese Communists in particular cases where that may serve our interests. We have dealt with it in relation to the Korean and Indo-China armistices. For nearly two years we have been, and still are, dealing with it in an effort to free our citizens and to obtain reciprocal renunciations of force.

But diplomatic recognition gives the recognized regime valuable rights and privileges, and, in the world of today, recognition by the United States gives the recipient much added prestige and influence at home and abroad.

Of course, diplomatic recognition is not to be withheld capriciously. In this matter, as others, the United States seeks to act in accordance with principles which contribute to a world society of order under law.

A test often applied is the ability of a regime actually to govern. But that is by no means a controlling factor. Nations often maintain diplomatic relations with governments-in-exile. And they frequently deny recognition to those in actual power.

Other customary tests are whether, as Thomas Jefferson put it, the recognized government reflects "the will of the nation, substantially declared"; whether the government conforms to the code of civilized nations, lives peacefully, and honors its international obligations.

Always, however, recognition is admitted to be an instrument of national policy, to serve enlightened self-interest.

One thing is established beyond a doubt. There is nothing automatic about recognition. It is never compelled by the mere lapse of time.

Another argument beginning to be heard is that diplomatic recognition is inevitable, so why not now?

First, let me say emphatically that the United States need never succumb to the argument of "inevitability." We, with our friends, can fashion our own destiny. We do not accept the mastery of Communist forces.

And let me go on to say: Communist-type despotisms are not so immutable as they sometimes appear. Time and circumstances work also upon them.

There is often an optical illusion which results from the fact that police states, supressing differences, give an external appearance of hard permanency, whereas the democracies, with their opposition parties and often speaking through different and discordant voices, seem the unstable, pliable members of the world society.

The reality is that a governmental system which tolerates diversity has a long life expectancy, whereas a system which seeks to impose conformity is always in danger. That results from the basic nature of human beings. Of all the arguments advanced for recognition of the Communist regime in China, the least cogent is the argument of "inevitability."

There are some who suggest that, if we assist the Chinese Communists to wax strong, then they will eventually break with Soviet Russia and that that is our best hope for the future.

No doubt, there are basic power rivalries between Russia and China in Asia. But also the Russian and Chinese Communist parties are bound together by close ideological ties.

Perhaps, if the ambitions of the Chinese Communists are inflated by successes, they might eventually clash with Soviet Russia.

Perhaps, too, if the Axis powers had won the Second World War, they would have fallen out among themselves.

But no one suggested that we should tolerate and even assist an Axis victory because in the end they would quarrel over the booty—of which we would be part.

We seek to appraise our China policies with an open mind and without emotion, except for a certain indignation at the prolonged and cruel abuse of American citizens in China. We have no feeling whatsoever that change is to be avoided merely in the interest of consistency or because change might be interpreted as admitting past error.

We always take into account the possibility of influencing the Communist regime to better ways if we had diplomatic relations with it, or if, without that, we had commercial and cultural contacts with it. But the experience of those who now recognize and deal with the Chinese Communist regime convinces us that, under present conditions, neither recognition, nor trade, nor cultural relations, nor all three, would favorably influence the evolution of affairs in China. The probable result, internally, would be the opposite of what we hope for.

Internationally the Chinese Communist regime does not conform to the practices of civilized nations; does not live up to its international obligations; has not been peaceful in the past and gives no evidence of being peaceful in the future. Its foreign policies are hostile to us and our Asian allies. Under these circumstances it would be folly for us to establish relations with the Chinese Communists which would enhance their ability to hurt us and our friends.

You may ask, "What of the future?" Are our policies merely negative? Do we see any prospect of resuming the many friendly ties, which, for many generations, the American people have had with the Chinese people and which we want to have again?

Do we see any chance that the potentially great Chinese nation, with its rich and ancient culture and wisdom, will again be able to play a constructive part in the councils of the nations?

We confidently answer these questions in the affirmative. Our confidence is based on certain fundamental beliefs. One is a belief in the future of human freedom. We know that the materialistic rule of international communism will never permanently serve the aspirations with which human beings are endowed by their Creator.

Within the Soviet Union the rulers have had to disavow Stalin's brand of communism.

Within the Soviet satellites even twelve years of indoctrination do not persuade the people that the Soviet system satisfies either their national or their individual desires.

Communism is repugnant to the Chinese people. They are, above all, individualists. We read the recent brave words uttered within Red China by the university lecturer: "To overthrow you cannot be called unpatriotic, because you Communists no longer serve the people."

We can confidently assume that international communism's rule of strict conformity is, in China as elsewhere, a passing and not a perpetual phase. We owe it to ourselves, our allies, and the Chinese people to do all that we can to contribute to that passing.

If we believed that this passing would be promoted by trade and cultural relations, then we would have such relations.

If we believed that this passing would be promoted by our having diplomatic relations with the present regime, then we would have such relations.

If we believed that this passing would be promoted by some participation of the present regime in the activities of the United Nations, then we would not oppose that.

We should be, and we are, constantly testing our policies, to be as certain as we can that, in the light of conditions as they from time to time are, our policies shall serve the great purposes to which our nation has been dedicated since its foundation—the cause of peace, justice, and human liberty.

Our polices are readily adjustable to meet the requirements of changing conditions. But there are occasions when not we but others should provide the change. Nothing could be more dangerous than for the United States to operate on the theory that, if hostile and evil forces do not quickly or readily change, then it is we who must change to meet them.

The United States exerts an immense influence in the world today, not only because it is powerful but because we stand for peace, for national independence, and personal liberty. Many free nations seek to coordinate their foreign policies with ours. Such coordination is indeed indispensable if the free world is to have the cohesion needed to make it safe. But United States policies will never serve as rallying points for free peoples if the impression is created that our policies are subject to change to meet Communist wishes for no reason other than that communism does not want to change. If communism is stubborn for the wrong, let us be steadfast for the right.

The capacity to change is an indispensable capacity. Equally indispensable is the capacity to hold fast that which is good. Given those qualities, we can hopefully look forward to the day when those in Asia who are yet free can confidently remain free and when the people of China and the people of America can resume their long history of cooperative friendship.

WORLD BROTHERHOOD IN A SPACE AGE [13]

ADLAI E. STEVENSON [14]

Adlai E. Stevenson gave these remarks in introducing Albert M. Greenfield at the World Brotherhood Dinner of the National Conference of Christians and Jews, in New York City, on Monday, November 11, 1957. Greenfield was for many years a real estate broker and banker of Philadelphia, prominent in Philadelphia and Pennsylvania philanthropy and general public service. He was awarded a distinguished service medal by the state of Pennsylvania in 1939 and was chairman of Committee of the American-Hebrew Awards for Better Understanding between Christians and Jews in America.

Stevenson during 1957 continued to speak with much frequency, displaying his qualities of leadership. He lectured before American universities and before many other bipartisan groups. He delivered a major address at Oxford University on May 24, 1957, when he was awarded the degree of honorary doctor of civil law. The public orator in awarding this degree conferred *honoris causa* offered, among other words of tribute, the declaration that "we see in him one who has never failed to exemplify those virtues which it is the duty of a university to foster, the passion for truth, sound learning spiced with charm, without rancor, eloquence without self-advertisement."

Stevenson's New York City appearance on Veterans' Day was followed by his three weeks of counseling with President Eisenhower and Secretary of State Dulles concerning the United States program for the NATO meeting on December 16 in Paris. The Democratic leader, to help with the bipartisan approach, had agreed to become a "consultant," but had refused to take part in drafting the proposals. On December 3 the President invited Stevenson to attend the Paris deliberations. The ex-presidential candidate immediately declined on the ground that he would be "without authority and necessarily identified with decisions I might not always agree with and could not publicly oppose."

In early 1958 Stevenson continued to loom up as a significant speaker and leader in Democratic national affairs, even though he was not generally regarded as a possible presidential nominee for a third time.[15]

---

[13] Text furnished with permission for this reprint through the courtesy of Adlai E. Stevenson.

[14] For biographical note, See Appendix.

[15] For further comment on Stevenson as a speaker see the Cumulative Author Index for references to his speeches in earlier volumes of *Representative American Speeches.*

I have here, if I may play just a little on a word, what I consider the perfect address for a meeting in behalf of World Brotherhood. It is the address on a letter that figured in Thornton Wilder's play *Our Town*. This is the address: "Jane Crofeet, the Crofeet Farm, Grover's Corners, Sutton County, New Hampshire, United States of America, Continent of North America, the Earth, the Solar System, the Universe, the Mind of God."

The address contains some truths the postman probably didn't appreciate. They are the truths we mark by our meeting here tonight: that we are all part of the one great company of mankind; that we are all residents in the one realm which knows no boundaries, no capitals, no foreign policy—for there are no foreigners; that we are all believers together in different prophets but in a single faith.

A hundred years ago, even fifty, perhaps even fifteen, to speak of World Brotherhood was, I suspect, to adorn with rhetoric what was at most a remote ideal. Today, however, it has become an insistent, demanding reality, thrust upon us whether we accept it or not by a science that has broken down the fences which had before separated the peoples of the world.

Last month a new star flashed across the skies. I wish it had been we who lighted that new star. It disturbs me greatly, as an American, that it was not. Yet I know, as a citizen of the world and as a member of tomorrow, that the basic issue is no longer the supremacy of nations. It is the supremacy of man for good or for evil, for survival or suicide. The significance of what has happened lies not in which nation has first reached into outer space but in the fact that man has now obliterated, for better or for worse, what we used to call time and distance.

I deny that the satellite is a portent of disaster. I think rather of John Donne's marking of the times in history that "are pregnant with those old twins, Hope and Fear." Surely this is such a time, a time not of catastrophe but of choice, not of disaster but of decision, a time when the preferment of our aspirations over our fears becomes the duty of citizenship in civilization.

A very large part, I suspect, of the maturing of mankind to its present estate has come from adversity, or the threat of adversity. More frontiers of what we call progress have probably been crossed under the pressure of necessity than by the power of reason. Prophets have appeared all through history to proclaim an ethic, but humanity has not heeded them, and the world has wandered its way—until the hard steel of survival itself has been pulled against our too soft mouths.

Now, once again, science has forced humanity to a crossroad from which there is no turning back, no escape—and just one road that leads upward. The choice is either extinction—or the human brotherhood that has been the vision of visionaries since the beginning of time.

I deny that human fulfillment cannot keep pace with material advance. We know and must insist rather that what was heralded by the splitting of the atom, what is now proclaimed by the earth satellite, is nothing narrower than man's complete genius—not to exterminate himself, but to control himself.

What that "bleep-bleep" is saying is that now the world has no option, that it must turn from narrow nationalism, sectarianism, racialism, that the only conceivable relationship among men is one based on men's full respect—yes, their love, if you please —for each other.

There is no cause for despair. There is only now a new imperative for peace—that we find that "great beat that is the heart of all human circumstances and of all human feeling."

Yet, to say, in effect, that now once again we have been driven forward by the pressure of crucial circumstances is no cause surely for satisfaction, no counsel of wisdom. If we have in the past been successful we have also been lucky. And surely the achievement of the brotherhood of man is not something to be left to the vagaries of chance or to the complacent, trusting hope that every new crisis may by some alchemy of fate be turned to humanity's good fortune.

It is my very great privilege and personal pleasure to represent you tonight in saluting a man whose precept it is that we cannot afford just to wait and to hope that everything will work out all right. By his deeds he has rejected the counsel that world brotherhood can win by a policy of brinksmanship, or that mankind can be safely merged by a series of shotgun—or shall we say, missile—marriages. This man's view is rather that world brotherhood must be worked for, prepared for, lived for and sought after with every resource at man's command.

Mr. Chairman, I have, in the discharge of my appointed duties on this occasion, made what we lawyers (you will pardon this brief "commercial") call a title search.

I find, and hereby certify to you, that Albert M. Greenfield is the holder of clear title to the status of rugged pioneer and devoted patron of world brotherhood. I find that he has, without regard to race, creed, color, or any other discernible line or distinction, taken active part in the most extraordinary variety of functions ever to come to my humble attention. I find that he has lent his name and services (and I suspect frequently something even more tangible) to the United Fund and the Community Chest, to the Philadelphia Symphony and to the Connie Mack Golden Jubilee Committee, to the Chapel of Four Chaplains and to the Army and Navy football games.

I can tell this group nothing of Albert Greenfield's contributions of mind and spirit and substance to the work of literally scores of organizations dedicated to the special service of what we call minority groups, and to the elimination of the false lines which mark minorities where there should be no divisions at all.

It is perhaps less well known that our guest of honor has been previously saluted by such various bodies as the Pen and Pencil Club and the Golden Slipper Square Club, the Veterans of Foreign Wars and the Chestnut Street Association, that the Keneseth Israel Men's Club has made him its "Man of the Year" and that he has been decorated by Pope Pius XI as a Commander in the Order of Pius IX.

My research, Mr. Chairman, has gone even to statistics. I am in a position to report, what I am sure Mr. Greenfield does not himself know—except perhaps with a kind of numbness— that there is record evidence of his participation, usually as chairman, in sixty-one committees, commissions, campaigns, chambers or celebrations; and of his previous receipt of twenty-nine honorary awards. The common denominator of most of this activity has been its reflection of this man's consuming belief in the dignity of man.

I note, Mr. Chairman, one lighter point. We speak of brotherhood as an all pervasive thing. Yet we appreciate its respect for one line. It asks of us that we bury all prejudice, every bias—except one. A Republican can in good conscience (I guess) be a Republican and (except in the suburbs) a Democrat. Mr. Chairman, I have said that there is *no* flaw in the brotherhood title of our honored guest. I advise you now that in 1928 he was a delegate from Pennsylvania to the National Convention of the Republican party. I advise you further that in 1948, 1952 and 1956 he was a Delegate-at-large from Pennsylvania to the national convention of the Democratic party. *This* is Brotherhood! And this is also *progress!*

(I might add that not only was Albert Greenfield a delegate to the 1956 convention. He was also a Democratic presidential elector. I claim the personal distinction of being the only living man who ever put Albert Greenfield out of a job.)

My friends, you will know that this indulgence of pleasantry only reflects the realization that virtually everything a grateful people can say to Albert Greenfield has been said before.

Yet we mark particularly tonight his most recent and perhaps most enduring contribution to the proposition that men are not only born equal but are entitled to live equal.

The Albert M. Greenfield Center for Human Relations at the University of Pennsylvania is living testament to the fact that today, more than ever before, the price of living is knowing. We cannot count, in the realm of human welfare, on being always the beneficiaries of scientific accomplishment. Nature is no longer man's master. It has become now man's servant. Because we have learned now to control some of the physical world we *must* hasten to learn to control ourselves. This Center for Human Relations is a pioneering step toward our studying now the ways of man and the laws of practical morality as deeply and as urgently as we have studied the ways of matter and the laws of nature.

By building this Center, Albert Greenfield has marked his faithfulness to what is written in the Talmud: "I did not find the world desolate when I entered it, and as my fathers planted for me, so do I plant for my children."

Ladies and gentlemen, acting for you, I confer the World Brotherhood Award Citation upon Albert M. Greenfield, Sugar Loaf, Chestnut Hill, Philadelphia, Pennsylvania, United States of America, Continent of North America, the Earth, the Solar System, the Universe, the Mind of God.

STATE OF THE UNION [16]

DWIGHT D. EISENHOWER [17]

President Dwight D. Eisenhower delivered this State of the Union address, his sixth, before the joint session of the Eighty-fifth Congress, Second Session, in the House of Representatives, on January 9, 1958.

The lawmakers, joined by Cabinet members, ambassadors and other diplomatic representatives, members of the Supreme Court, and gallery visitors, made up the audience of some five hundred on the floor and eight hundred in the galleries. The President's gallery guests included Mrs. Eisenhower.

At 12:31 the President was escorted into the chamber. The audience rose and applauded for two minutes. Vice President Nixon was seated on the rostrum with Speaker Sam Rayburn.

The ovation no doubt was partly stimulated both by the pervading sense of national crisis and by the reassurance of the President's renewal of physical vigor after his mild stroke of November 25.

The President moved briskly and smilingly to the lectern and stood with uplifted arms in response to the acclaim. He was erect, vigorous, with few or no signs of invalidism. He read the five-thousand-word speech with undiminished surety and audience projection. With only minor deviations, he followed the typed script on which the key sentences were heavily underlined. He used no gestures. He carefully placed each completed page in a pile beside the unread ones. Here and there he stumbled over syllables, but had no noticeable speech impairment. His articulation was much as it had been in his earlier White House public utterances. He spoke deliberately with special emphasis on the section dealing with peace.

The President's report dealt exclusively with our military policies. What in 1958 should we do in this cold war to offset the Soviet Union's space program? Forthrightly the President acknowledged that the Soviets were "probably" ahead of this country in the missile race and that the American people had not anticipated the tremendous psychological effect of the Suptniks. His central theme was "to insure our safety through strength," and also to take other steps for "if we did only this the future would hold nothing for the world but an age of terror."

This central theme expanded into an eight-point program requiring "imperative" action. He proposed (1) a reorganization of the Defense

[16] From the *Congressional Record*. 104:171-5. January 9, 1958. The text was also compared with that printed in the New York *Times* for January 10 and found to be substantially the same. The *Congressional Record* text (unlike the *Times* report) included the applause.

[17] For biographical note, see Appendix.

Department, (2) stepped-up atomic-age defense, (3) more effective foreign aid, (4) increased foreign trade, (5) exchange of atomic secrets with our allies, (6) increased spending for education and research, (7) efforts to maintain a balanced budget, and (8) closer cooperation with Russia on a "science for peace" program. The first seven of these programs would require legislation.

What was the reception by his audience? The President was applauded some forty times during his forty-three-minute speech. Most of this enthusiastic approval was from the Republicans of this Democratic-controlled Congress. The preliminary and concluding ovations, however, were spontaneous and unanimous.

Criticism was immediate. The address was held to offer only broad formulas, practically none of them new. Some proposals were "too little or too late." The message allegedly lacked the decisive leadership that Theodore or Franklin D. Roosevelt would have voiced in such emergency. The critics noted that the Administration was three months late in responding to the Sputnik challenges, and much later in setting up a program to meet the missile threat. The sense of urgency, it was said, seemed to be lacking. And the successive sections moved toward relative unimpressiveness. The "Works of Peace" were alleged to constitute a perfunctory anticlimax.

Chiefly the critics waited to see whether the President would take decisive leadership in reorganizing the military establishment to achieve unity in defense activity. Rough going in Congress was in prospect for most of the eight proposals. Certainly the House and Senate would go all out for defense. But foreign aid, reduction of tariffs, sharing of atomic secrets, and even increased spending for education and research would all be sharply debated and probably would not be translated into policy in harmony with the President's will and expectancy.

The speech, nevertheless, was one of the two or three best of Eisenhower's during his term of office. It well dramatized for this nation and the world the most important issues before the United States at the outset of 1958.[18]

Mr. President, Mr. Speaker, Members of the Eighty-fifth Congress, my fellow-citizens:

It is again my high privilege to extend personal greetings to the members of the Eighty-fifth Congress.

Moreover, Mrs. Eisenhower would like to join me in wishing for you and your families a bright and prosperous New Year.

And because of the felicitous circumstances that the birth anniversaries of our Speaker and our Vice President occur this

[18] For further comment on Eisenhower as a speaker, see the Cumulative Author Index for references to his speeches in earlier volumes of *Representative American Speeches*.

same week, I know all of us will join in saying to both: Happy Birthday!

Now, my friends, honest men differ in their appraisal of America's material and intellectual strength, and the dangers that today confront us. But all know that these dangers are real.

The purpose of this message is to outline the measures that can give the American people a confidence—just as real—in their own security.

I am not here to justify the past, to gloss over the problems of the present, or propose any easy solutions for the future.

I am here to state what I believe to be right, what I believe to be wrong; and to propose action for correcting what I think wrong!

I

There are two tasks confronting us that so far outweigh all others that I shall devote this year's message entirely to them.

The first is to insure our safety through strength.

As to our strength, I have repeatedly voiced this conviction: we now have a broadly based and efficient defensive strength, including a great deterrent power, which is, for the present, our best guarantee against war; but unless we act wisely and promptly, we could lose that capacity to deter attack or defend ourselves.

My profoundest conviction is that the American people will say, as one man: No matter what the exertions or sacrifices, we shall maintain that necessary strength!

But we could make no more tragic mistake than merely to concentrate on military strength.

For if we did only this, the future would hold nothing for the world but an Age of Terror.

And so our second task is to do the constructive work of building a genuine peace. [*Applause*] We must never become so preoccupied with our desire for military strength that we neglect those areas of economic development, trade, diplomacy, education, ideas and principles where the foundations of real peace must be laid. [*Applause*]

II

The threat to our safety, and to the hope of a peaceful world, can be simply stated. It is Communist imperialism.

This threat is not something imagined by critics of the Soviets. Soviet spokesmen, from the beginning, have publicly and frequently declared their aim to expand their power, one way or another, throughout the world.

The threat has become increasingly serious as this expansionist aim has been reinforced by an advancing industrial, military and scientific establishment.

But what makes the Soviet threat unique in history is its all-inclusiveness. Every human activity is pressed into service as a weapon of expansion. Trade, economic development, military power, arts, science, education, the whole world of ideas—all are harnessed to this same chariot of expansion.

The Soviets are, in short, waging total cold war.

The only answer to a regime that wages total cold war is to wage total peace. [Applause]

This means bringing to bear every asset of our personal and national lives upon the task of building the conditions in which security and peace can grow.

III

Among our assets, let us first briefly glance at our military power.

Military power serves the cause of security by making prohibitive the cost of any aggressive attack.

It serves the cause of peace by holding up a shield behind which the patient constructive work of peace can go on.

But it can serve neither cause if we make either of two mistakes. The one would be to overestimate our strength, and thus neglect crucially important actions in the period just ahead. The other would be to underestimate our strength. Thereby we might be tempted to become irresolute in our foreign relations, to dishearten our friends, and to lose our national poise and perspective in approaching the complex problems ahead.

Any orderly balance sheet of military strength must be in two parts. The first is the position as of today. The second is the position in the period ahead.

As of today, our defensive shield comprehends a vast complex of ground, sea, and air units, superbly equipped and strategically deployed around the world. The most powerful deterrent to war in the world today lies in the retaliatory power of our Strategic Air Command and the aircraft of our Navy. They present to any potential attacker who would unleash war upon the world the prospect of virtual annihilation of his own country.

Even if we assume a surprise attack on our bases, with a marked reduction in our striking power, our bombers would immediately be on their way in sufficient strength to accomplish this mission of retaliation. Every informed government knows this. It is no secret.

Since the Korean armistice, the American people have spent $225 billion in maintaining and strengthening this over-all defensive shield.

This is the position as of today.

Now, as to the period ahead: Every part of our Military Establishment must and will be equipped to do its defensive job with the most modern weapons and methods. But it is particularly important to our planning that we make a candid estimate of the effect of long-range ballistic missiles on the present deterrent power I have described.

At this moment, the consensus of opinion is that we are probably somewhat behind the Soviets in some areas of long-range ballistic missile development. But it is my conviction, based on close study of all relevant intelligence, with the best information that scientists can bring to me, that if we make the necessary effort, we will have the missiles, in the needed quantity and in time, to sustain and strengthen the deterrent power of our increasingly efficient bombers. [Applause] One encouraging fact evidencing this ability is the rate of progress we have achieved since we began to concentrate on these missiles.

The intermediate ballistic missiles, Thor and Jupiter, have already been ordered into production. The parallel progress in the intercontinental ballistic missile effort will be advanced by new plans for acceleration. The development of the submarine-based Polaris missile system has progressed so well that its future procurement schedules are being moved forward markedly.

When it is remembered that our country has concentrated on the development of ballistic missiles for only about a third as long as the Soviets, these achievements show a rate of progress that speaks for itself. [Applause] Only a brief time back, we were spending at the rate of only about $1 million a year on long range ballistic missiles. In 1957 we spent more than $1 billion on the Atlas, Titan, Thor, Jupiter, and Polaris programs. This is a rate of increase of one thousand times.

But I repeat, gratifying though the rate of progress is, we must still do more.

Our real problem, then, is not our strength today; it is rather the vital necessity of action today to insure our strength tomorrow.

What I have just said applies to our strength as a single country. But we are not alone. I have returned from the recent NATO meeting with renewed conviction that, because we are a part of a worldwide community of free and peaceful nations, our own security is immeasurably increased. [Applause]

By contrast, the Soviet Union has surrounded itself with captive and sullen nations. Like a crack in the crust of an uneasily sleeping volcano, the Hungarian uprising revealed the depth and intensity of the patriotic longing for liberty that still burns within these countries. [Applause]

The world thinks of us as a country which is strong, but which will never start a war. The world also thinks of us as a land which has never enslaved anyone and which is animated by humane ideals. This friendship, based on common ideals, is one of our greatest sources of strength.

It cements into a cohesive security arrangement the aggregate of the spiritual, military, and economic strength of all those nations which, with us, are allied by treaties and agreements.

Up to this point I have talked almost solely about our military strength to deter a possible future war.

I now want to talk about the strength we need to win a different kind of a war—one that has already been launched against us.

It is the intensive economic offensive that has been mounted by the Communist imperialists against free nations.

The Communist imperialist regimes have for some time been largely frustrated in their attempts at expansion based directly on force. As a result, they have begun to concentrate heavily on economic penetration, particularly of newly developing countries, as a preliminary to political domination.

This nonmilitary drive, if underestimated, could defeat the free world regardless of our military strength. This danger is all the greater precisely because many of us fail or refuse to recognize it. Thus, some people may be tempted to finance our extra military effort by cutting economic assistance. But at the very time when the economic threat is assuming menacing proportions, to fail to strengthen our own effort would be nothing less than reckless folly. [Applause]

Admittedly, most of us did not anticipate the intensity of the psychological impact upon the world of the launching of the first earth satellite. Let us not make the same kind of mistake in another field, by failing to anticipate the much more serious impact of the Soviet economic offensive.

As with our military potential, our economic assets are more than equal to the task. Our independent farmers produce an abundance of food and fiber. Our free workers are versatile, intelligent, and hard working. Our businessmen are imaginative and resourceful. The productivity, the adaptability of the American economy is the solid foundation stone of our whole security structure.

We have just concluded another prosperous year. Our output was once more the greatest in the nation's history. In the latter part of the year, some decline in employment and output occurred, following the exceptionally rapid expansion of recent years. In a free economy, reflecting as it does the independent judgments of millions of people, growth typically moves forward unevenly. But the basic forces of growth remain unimpaired. There are solid grounds for confidence that economic growth will be resumed without an extended interruption. [*Applause*] Moreover, the Federal Government, constantly alert to signs of weakening in any part of our economy, always stands ready, with its full power, to take any appropriate further action to promote renewed business expansion.

If our history teaches us anything, it is this lesson: So far as the economic potential of our nation is concerned, the believers in the future of America have always been the realists. [*Applause*]

I count myself as one of this company.

Our long-range problem, then, is not the stamina of our enormous engine of production. Our problem is to make sure that we use these vast economic forces confidently and creatively, not only in direct military defense efforts, but likewise in our foreign policy, through such activities as mutual economic aid and foreign trade.

In much the same way, we have tremendous potential resources on other nonmilitary fronts to help in countering the Soviet threat: education, science, research, and, not least, the ideas and principles by which we live. And in all these cases the task ahead is to bring these resources more sharply to bear upon the new tasks of security and peace in a swiftly changing world.

IV

There are many items in the Administration's program of a kind frequently included in a State of the Union message. They will be the subjects of later messages to the Congress. Today I speak only about matters bearing directly upon our security and peace.

I now place before you an outline of action designed to focus our resources upon the two tasks of security and peace.

In this special category I list eight items requiring prompt action. They are not merely desirable. They are imperative.

1. *Defense Reorganization*

The first need is to assure ourselves that military organization facilitates rather than hinders the functioning of the Military

Establishment in maintaining the security of the nation. [*Applause*]

Since World War II, the purpose of achieving maximum organizational efficiency in a modern Defense Establishment has several times occasioned action by the Congress and by the Executive.

The advent of revolutionary new devices, bringing with them the problem of over-all continental defense, creates new difficulties, reminiscent of those attending the advent of the airplane more than a half century ago.

Some of the important new weapons which technology has produced do not fit into any existing service pattern. They cut across all services, involve all services, and transcend all services, at every stage from development to operation. In some instances they defy classification according to branch of service.

Unfortunately, the uncertainties resulting from such a situation, and the jurisdictional disputes attending upon it, tend to bewilder and confuse the public and create the impression that service differences are damaging the national interest.

Let us by all means proudly remember that the members of the Armed Forces give their basic allegiance solely to the United States. [*Applause*] Of that fact, all of us are certain. But pride of service and mistaken zeal in promoting particular doctrine has more than once occasioned the kind of difficulty of which I have just spoken.

I am not attempting today to pass judgment on the charge of harmful service rivalries. But one thing is sure. Whatever they are, America wants them stopped. [*Applause*]

Recently I have had under special study, with the intimate association of Secretary McElroy, the never-ending problem of efficient organization, complicated as it is by new weapons. Soon my own conclusions will be finalized. I shall promptly take such Executive action as is necessary and, in a separate message, I shall present appropriate recommendations to the Congress.

Meanwhile, without anticipating the detailed form that a reorganization should take, I can state its main lines in terms of objectives:

A major purpose of military organization is to achieve real unity in the Defense Establishment in all the principal features of military activity. Of all these, one of the most important to our nation's security is strategic planning and direction. This work must be done under unified direction.

The Defense Establishment must plan for a better integration of its defensive resources, particularly with repect to the newer weapons now building and under development. These obviously require full coordination in their development, production, and use. Good organization can help assure such coordination.

In recognition of the need for single control in some of our most advanced development projects, the Secretary of Defense has already decided to concentrate into one organization all the antimissile and satellite technology undertaken within the Department of Defense.

Another requirement of military organization is a clear sub-ordination of the military services to duly constituted civilian authority. [*Applause*] This control must be real; not merely on the surface.

Next there must be assurance that an excessive number of compartments in organization will not create costly and confusing compartments in our scientific and industrial effort.

Finally, to end interservice disputes requires clear organization and decisive central direction, supported by the unstinted cooperation of every individual in the Defense Establishment, civilian and military.

2. *Accelerated Defense Effort*

The second major action item is the acceleration of the defense effort in particular areas affected by the fast pace of scientific and technological advance.

Some of the points at which improved and increased effort are most essential are these:

We must have sure warning in case of any attack. The improvement of warning equipment is becoming increasingly important as we approach the period when long-range missiles will come into use.

We must protect and disperse our striking forces and increase their readiness for instant reaction. This means more base facilities and more standby crews.

We must maintain deterrent retaliatory power. This means, among other things, stepped-up, long-range missile programs; accelerated programs for other effective missile systems; and, for some years, more advanced aircraft.

We must maintain freedom of the seas. This means nuclear submarines and cruisers; improved antisubmarine weapons; missile ships; and the like.

We must maintain all necessary types of mobile forces to deal with local conflicts, should there be need. This means further improvements in equipment, mobility, tactics, and fire-power.

Through increases in pay and incentive, we must maintain in the Armed Forces the skilled manpower modern military forces require. [Applause]

We must be forward looking in our research and development to anticipate and achieve the unimagined weapons of the future.

With these and other improvements, we intend to assure that our vigilance, power, and technical excellence keep abreast of any realistic threat we face.

3. Mutual Aid

Third. We must continue to strengthen our mutual-security efforts.

Most people now realize that our program of military aid and defense support are an integral part of our own defense effort. If the foundations of the free world structure were progressively allowed to crumble under the pressure of Communist imperialism, the entire house of freedom would be in danger of collapse.

As for the mutual economic assistance program, the benefit to us is threefold: First, the countries receiving this aid become bulwarks against Communist encroachment as their military defenses and economies are strengthened. Nations that are conscious of a steady improvement in their industry, education, health, and standard of living are not apt to fall prey to the blandishments of Communist imperialists; second, these countries are helped to reach the point where mutually profitable trade can expand between them and us; third, the mutual confidence that comes from working together on constructive projects creates an atmosphere in which real understanding and peace can flourish.

To help bring these multiple benefits, our economic aid effort should be made more effective.

In proposals for future economic aid, I am stressing a greater use of repayable loans, through the development loan fund, through funds generated by sale of surplus farm products, and through the Export-Import Bank.

While some increase in Government funds will probably be required, it remains our objective to encourage shifting to the use of private capital sources as rapidly as possible.

My friends, one great obstacle to the economic aid program in the past has been, not a rational argument against it on the merits, but a catchword: "give-away program."

The fact is that no investment we make in our own security can pay us greater dividends than necessary amounts of economic aid to friendly nations.

This is no "give-away."

Let's stick to facts!

We cannot afford to have one of our most essential security programs shot down with a slogan!

4. *Mutual Trade*

Now fourth: Both in our national interest, and in the interest of world peace, we must have a five-year extension of the trade agreements act—with broadened authority to negotiate.

World trade supports a significant segment of American industry and agriculture. It provides employment for 4.5 million American workers. It provides the opportunity for American free enterprise to develop on a worldwide scale. It strengthens our friends and increases their desire to be friends. World trade helps to lay the groundwork for peace by making all free nations of the world stronger and more self-reliant.

America is today the world's greatest trading nation. If we use this great asset wisely to meet the expanding demands of the world, we shall not only provide future opportunities for our own business, agriculture and labor, but in the process strengthen our security posture and other prospects for a prosperous, harmonious world.

As President McKinley said, as long ago as 1901:

"Isolation is no longer possible or desirable. . . . The period of exclusiveness is past."

5. *Scientific Cooperation With Our Allies*

Fifth: It is highly important that the Congress enact the necessary legislation to enable us to exchange appropriate scientific and technical information with friendly countries.

It is wasteful in the extreme for friendly allies to consume talent and money in solving problems that their friends have already solved—all because of artificial barriers to sharing. And we cannot afford to cut ourselves off from the brilliant talents and minds of scientists in friendly countries. The task ahead will be hard enough without handcuffs of our own making.

The groundwork for this kind of cooperation has already been laid in discussions among NATO countries. Promptness in following through with legislation will be the best possible evidence of American unity of purpose in cooperating with our friends.

6. *Education and Research*

In the area of education and research, I recommend a balanced program to improve our resources, involving an investment of about a billion dollars over a four-year period. This involves new activities by the Department of Health, Education and Welfare designed to encourage improved teaching quality and student opportunities in the interests of national security. It also provides a five-fold increase in the sums available to the National Science Foundation for its activities in stimulating and improving science education.

Scrupulous attention has been paid to maintaining local control of educational policy, spurring the maximum amount of local efforts, and to avoiding undue stress on the physical sciences at the expense of other branches of learning.

In the field of research, I am asking for substantial increases in basic research funds, including a doubling of the funds available to the National Science Foundation for this purpose.

But Federal action can do only a part of the job. In both education and research, redoubled exertions will be necessary on the part of all Americans if we are to rise to the demands of our times. This means hard work on the part of state and local governments, private industries, schools and colleges, private organizations and foundations, teachers, parents, and—perhaps most important of all—the student himself, with his bag of books and his homework.

With this kind of all-inclusive campaign, we can create the intellectual capital we need for the years ahead—and do all this, not as regimented pawns, but as free men and women!

7. *Spending and Saving*

Seventh: To provide for this effort for security, we must apply stern tests of priority to other expenditures, both military and civilian.

This extra effort involves, most immediately, the need for a supplemental defense appropriation of $1.3 billion for fiscal year 1958.

In the 1959 budget, increased expenditures for missiles, nuclear ships, atomic energy, research and development, science and education, a special contingency fund to deal with possible new technological discoveries, and increases in pay and incentives to obtain and retain competent manpower add up to a total increase over the comparable figures in the 1957 budget of about $4 billion.

I believe that, in spite of these necessary increases, we should strive to finance the 1959 security effort out of expected revenues. While we now believe that expected revenues and expenditures will roughly balance, our real purpose will be to achieve adequate security, but always with the utmost regard for efficiency and careful management.

This purpose will require the cooperation of Congress in making careful analysis of estimates presented; it means reducing expenditures on less essential military programs and installations, postponing some new civilian programs, transferring some to the states, and curtailing or eliminating others.

Such related matters as the national debt ceiling and tax revenues will be dealt with in later messages.

8. *Works of Peace*

Now my last call for action is not primarily addressed to the Congress and people of the United States. Rather, it is a message from the people of the United States to all other peoples, especially those of the Soviet Union.

This is the spirit of what we Americans would like to say:

"In the last analysis, there is only one solution to the grim problems that lie ahead. The world must stop the present plunge toward more and more destructive weapons of war, and turn the corner that will start our steps firmly on the path toward lasting peace.

"Our greatest hope for success lies in a universal fact: the people of the world, as people, have always wanted peace and want peace now.

"The problem, then, is to find a way of translating this universal desire into action.

"This will require more than words of peace. It requires works of peace."

Now, may I try to give you some concrete examples of the kind of works of peace that might make a beginning in the new direction.

For a start our people should learn to know each other better. Recent negotiations in Washington have provided a basis in principle for greater freedom of communication and exchange of people. I urge the Soviet Government to cooperate in turning principle into practice by prompt and tangible actions that will break down the unnatural barriers that have blocked the flow of thought and understanding between our people.

Another kind of work of peace is cooperation on projects of human welfare. For example, we now have it within our power to eradicate from the face of the earth that age-old scourge of mankind: malaria. We are embarking with other nations in an all-out five-year campaign to blot out this curse forever. We invite the Soviets to join with us in this great work of humanity.

Indeed, we would be willing to pool our efforts with the Soviets in other campaigns against the diseases that are the common enemy of all mortals—such as cancer and heart disease.

If people can get together on such projects, is it not possible that we could then go on to a full-scale cooperative program of science for peace?

A program of science for peace might provide a means of funneling into one place the results of research from scientists everywhere and from there making it available to all parts of the world.

There is almost no limit to the human betterment that could result from such cooperation. Hunger and disease could increasingly be driven from the earth. The age-old dream of a good life for all could, at long last, be translated into reality. [Applause]

But of all the works of peace, none is more needed now than a real first step toward disarmament. [Applause]

Last August the United Nations General Assembly, by an overwhelming vote, approved a disarmament plan that we and our allies sincerely believed to be fair and practical. The Soviets have rejected both the plan and the negotiating procedure set up by the United Nations. As a result, negotiation on this supremely important issue is now at a standstill.

But the world cannot afford to stand still on disarmament. [Applause] We must never give up the search for a basis of agreement.

Our allies from time to time develop differing ideas on how to proceed. We must concert these convictions among ourselves. Thereafter, any reasonable proposal that holds promise for disarmament and reduction of tension must be heard, discussed, and, if possible, negotiated. [Applause]

There is one indispensable condition. A disarmanent proposal, to hold real promise, must at the minimum have one feature: reliable means to insure compliance by all. It takes actions and demonstrated integrity on both sides to create and sustain confidence. And confidence in a genuine disarmament agreement is vital, not only to the signers of the agreement, but also to the millions of people all over the world who are weary of tensions and armaments.

I say once more, to all peoples, that we will always go the extra mile with anyone on earth if it will bring us nearer a genuine peace. [Applause]

Conclusion

These, then, are the ways in which we must funnel our energies more efficiently into the task of advancing security and peace.

These actions demand and expect two things of the American people: sacrifice, and a high degree of understanding. For sacrifice to be effective it must be intelligent. Sacrifice must be made for the right purpose and in the right place—even if that place happens to come close to home.

After all, it is no good demanding sacrifice in general terms one day, and the next day, for local reasons, opposing the elimination of some unneeded Federal facility. [Applause]

It is pointless to condemn Federal spending in general, and the next moment condemn just as strongly an effort to reduce the particular Federal grant that touches one's own interest.

And it makes no sense whatever to spend additional billions on military strength to deter a potential danger, and then, by cutting aid and trade programs, let the world succumb to a present danger in economic guise. [Applause]

My friends of the Congress: The world is waiting to see how wisely and decisively a free representative government can and will now act.

I believe that this Congress possesses and will display the wisdom promptly to do its part in translating into law the actions demanded by our nation's interests. But, to make law effective, our kind of government needs the full voluntary support of millions of Americans for these actions.

I am fully confident that the response of the Congress and of the American people will make this time of test a time of honor. Mankind then will see more clearly than ever that the future belongs, not to the concept of the regimented atheistic state, but to the people—the God-fearing, peace-loving people of all the world. [*Applause, the Members rising*]

PERSONALITIES

PORTRAITS OF FIVE SENATORS IN THE
SENATE RECEPTION ROOM [1]

JOHN F. KENNEDY [2]

Senator John F. Kennedy (Democrat, Massachusetts), chairman of the Committee, gave this address before the Senate, on May 1, 1957, "pursuant to the filing with the Senate the final report of the Special Committee recommending five senators whose portraits are to be placed in the Senate Reception Room."

The other Committee members were Senators Richard B. Russell of Georgia, Mike Mansfield of Montana, John W. Bricker of Ohio, and Styles Bridges of New Hampshire.

The Senator briefly outlined the distinction of each of the five Senators named: Henry Clay, Daniel Webster, John C. Calhoun, Robert M. La Follette, Sr., and Robert A. Taft. He added: "Speaking only for myself, I will say to the Senate that I had the most difficulty in excluding from the list three other outstanding senators of the past." The three were George Norris of Nebraska, Thomas Hart Benton of Missouri, and Oliver Ellsworth of Connecticut.

Senator Kennedy also listed a dozen others high on the list of those nominated. He then analyzed and defended at length the five chosen. (This editor regrets that the limits of this annual volume prevent the inclusion of the entire address, which, with senatorial comments, occupied some two hours.)

Following Kennedy's speech, Senators Everett Saltonstall of Massachusetts and Norris Cotton of New Hampshire eulogized Webster; Thruston Morton of Kentucky, Clay; Strom Thurmond of South Carolina, Calhoun; John Bricker of Ohio, La Follette; and Frank Lausche of Ohio, Taft.

The Kennedy speech constituted a series of eulogies, to be examined with profit by students interested in the important speeches of tribute in American political history—for example, that of Woodrow Wilson at the birthplace of Lincoln, at Hodgenville, Kentucky.

Students of American public address have long placed Clay, Calhoun, and Webster in the forefront of effective Senate leaders in debate. The editor of this volume would add, among the other fifteen that Kennedy

[1] Text supplied by Senator John F. Kennedy. The speech was also printed in the *Congressional Record.* 103:5548-57 (daily edition). May 1, 1957.

[2] For biographical note, see Appendix.

listed, Senators George Norris of Nebraska, Thomas Benton of Missouri, William E. Borah of Idaho, and Stephen Douglas of Illinois. Others on the committee's preferred list included Alben Barkley of Kentucky, Carter Glass of Virginia, Oscar Underwood of Alabama, Arthur Vandenberg of Michigan, Robert Wagner of New York, and Thomas Walsh of Montana. These, however, like Taft, were so recent as to bring into question the historical perspective of the selection committee.

Kennedy, in 1957 and 1958, continued to impress the nation and his numerous Democratic audiences with his abilities as speaker, thinker, and personality. His *Profiles in Courage* continued to be widely read and quoted.[3]

Mr. President:

As Chairman of the Special Senate Committee on the Senate Reception Room, established by Senate Resolution 145 of the 84th Congress as amended, I wish to report to the Senate that our Committee has completed its deliberations, and its surveys of scholarly and senatorial opinion as described in the Committee Report, and recommends that there be placed in the five unfilled spaces in the Senate Reception Room paintings portraying the following five outstanding Senators of the past:

Senator Henry Clay, of Kentucky, who served in the Senate 1806-07, 1810-11, 1831-42, 1849-52. Resourceful expert in the art of the possible, his fertile mind, persuasive voice, skillful politics and tireless energies were courageously devoted to the reconciliation of conflict between North and South, East and West, capitalism and agrarianism. A political leader who put the national good above party, a spokesman for the West whose love for the Union outweighed sectional pressures, he acquired more influence and more respect as responsible leader of the loyal but ardent opposition than many who occupied the White House. His adroit statesmanship and political finesse in times of national crisis demonstrated the values of intelligent compromise in a Federal democracy, without impairing either his convictions or his courage to stand by them.

Senator Daniel Webster, of Massachusetts, who served in the Senate 1827-41, 1845-50. Eloquent and articulate champion of "Liberty *and* Union, now and forever, one and inseparable," he

[3] For further comment on Kennedy as a speaker, see *Representative American Speeches: 1956-57,* p 165-172, "The Intellectual and the Politician."

grasped in an age of divided loyalties the full meaning of the American Constitution and of the supremacy and indissolubility of the national government. Molding the symbols of the Union he cherished so strongly that neither secession nor war could break them, his steadfast courage and powerful leadership in two of the Senate's most historic and critical debates were brilliantly portrayed in orations attentively heard and eagerly read. Influential spokesman for industrial expansion, his dedication to Union above all personal and partisan considerations overshadowed the petty moral insensitivities which never compromised his national principles; and his splendid dignity and decorum elevated the status and prestige of the Senate.

Senator John C. Calhoun, of South Carolina, who served in the Senate 1832-43, 1845-50. Forceful logician of state sovereignty, masterful defender of the rights of a political minority against the dangers of an unchecked majority, his profoundly penetrating and original understanding of the social bases of government has significantly influenced American political theory and practice. Sincerely devoted to the public good as he saw it, the ultimate tragedy of his final cause neither detracts from the greatness of his leadership nor tarnishes his efforts to avert bloodshed. Outspoken yet respected, intellectual yet beloved, his leadership on every major issue in that critical era of transition significantly shaped the role of the Senate and the destiny of the nation.

Senator Robert M. La Follette, Sr., of Wisconsin, who served in the Senate 1906-25. Ceaseless battler for the underprivileged in an age of special privilege, courageous independent in an era of partisan conformity, he fought memorably against tremendous odds and stifling inertia for social and economic reforms which ultimately proved essential to American progress in the twentieth century. Determined to make law serve the rights of persons as well as property, to make government serve the interests of great social justice as well as great political parties, his constructive pioneering efforts to promote the general welfare aroused the slumbering conscience of the nation and made the Senate more responsive to it. The bitter antagonisms stirred by his unyielding opposition to international commitments and conflict were ultimately submerged by widespread admiration for his dedicated life-long fight against political corruption and corporate greed.

Senator Robert A. Taft, of Ohio, who served in the Senate 1939-53. The conscience of the conservative movement, its ablest exponent and most constructive leader, his high integrity, analytical mind and sheer industry quickly won him a select spot in the councils of his party and the hearts of all his colleagues. His Senate leadership transcended partisanship; his political courage and candor put principles above ambition. Dedicated to the Constitution and the American tradition of individual rights as his keen legal mind interpreted them, he demonstrated the importance of a balanced and responsible opposition in an age of powerful governments.

These five names, it should be made clear, and I shall discuss some of the objections raised to each in a moment, are not offered as "the five greatest" senators of all time. The Senate resolution under which we were deliberating instead called for simply—

five outstanding persons from among all persons, but not a living person, who have served as Members of the Senate since the formation of the Government.

Nevertheless, the decisions of the Special Committee in agreeing to these five names were unanimous. And although we recognize, with humility, the hazards of attempting to pass judgment on other members of the Senate, when we claim for ourselves neither the detachment nor the expertness of professional historians—and although we recognize further that no other senator or committee of senators would have necessarily reached the same conclusions—we can take pride nevertheless in the fact that Clay, Webster, Calhoun, and La Follette were among the top five receiving the most endorsements from our panel of 150 scholars; that the same four names were also among the top five receiving the most endorsements from those senators who responded to our inquiry; and that the late Senator Taft, whose name completes the five recommended by our Committee, was the first choice of the senators who responded and among the first ten in the poll of scholars.

Our Committee does not, of course, attempt to say that many other senators of the past are not deserving of recognition, or are not considered, in the minds of some, even "greater," however that term may be measured. On the contrary, the excellence of so many nominations made our assignment a nearly impossible task. Speaking only for myself, I will say to the Senate that I had the most difficulty excluding from the list three other outstanding Senators of the past:

George Norris, of Nebraska, one of the most courageous, dedicated men ever to sit in the Senate, and one whose influence on the public power, agricultural, labor and political aspects of this nation will long endure;

Thomas Hart Benton, of Missouri, the great "Nestor of the Senate" from 1820 to 1850, who on more than one occasion took on the Great Triumvirate individually and collectively and bested them in the Senate itself; and

Oliver Ellsworth, of Connecticut, the outstanding figure in the first Senate, who authored the Federal Judiciary Act that will always remain a monument to his genius and shepherded the Bill of Rights through the Senate.

Many others deserve recognition, and were the subjects of scholarly, thoughtful letters from members of the Senate or distinguished historians, political scientists and public figures. Sports writers choosing entrants to Baseball's Hall of Fame in Cooperstown have it easy by comparison—for them, and for those who miss, there will always be a next year. Our Committee was limited to five—for all time—without a "next year," a "second team," or a list of those deserving "honorable mention."

Nevertheless, in the Report filed today, the Committee lists in alphabetical order the following names (omitting the three I have already mentioned), which were among those most prominently mentioned in letters received by the Committee from members of the Senate, our panel of scholars, and the general public, which we list because of our regret that a selection of only five names was permitted and because of the possibility that some future committee of the Senate, meeting at some future date, will find occasion to honor additional names:

Alben W. Barkley, of Kentucky
William Borah, of Idaho
Stephen Douglas, of Illinois
Carter Glass, of Virginia
Justin Smith Morrill, of Vermont
John Sherman, of Ohio
Charles Sumner, of Massachusetts
Lyman Trumbull, of Illinois
Oscar Underwood, of Alabama
Arthur Vandenberg, of Michigan
Robert Wagner, of New York
Thomas Walsh, of Montana

The members of the Special Committee recognized that they faced a particular problem with respect to senators of the twentieth century. We realize that many of those nominated from this period were men with whom contemporary senators, including members of the Committee, have served, and about whom both sentiment and prejudice may still exist in sufficient quantity to influence the opinions of senators, historians, and the general public. Nevertheless, the mandate of the Senate as contained in Senate Resolution 145 called for the selection to be made "from among all persons . . . who have served as members of the Senate since the formation of the Government"; and this clearly implied that, to the extent possible, the entire history of the Senate should be considered and represented in the selection process. It is important to note, moreover, that to eliminate consideration of twentieth century senators and thus to impose a cutoff date of 1900 may well have meant imposing in effect a cutoff date of approximately 1850, because of the predominance of outstanding senators from the period of 1830 to 1850 compared with those in the latter half of the century. To have recommended five senators who all served more than a century ago would not, we finally decided, fulfill either the mandate of the Senate Resolution or our efforts to arouse public interest in the Senate, its greatness and its role.

With this in mind, the Committee has selected Senators Robert M. La Follette, Sr., of Wisconsin and Robert A. Taft of Ohio as outstanding representatives of the progressive and conservative movements in the twentieth century. We realize, of course, that considerable controversy and sentiment still surround each of them; that it is impossible to prove that they deserve the honor more than Norris or Vandenberg, for example, or Borah, Carter Glass, Barkley, Wagner, Walsh, Underwood or any among a dozen others who were seriously considered; and that whatever names are chosen from the twentieth century will appear to suffer in comparison with the Great Triumvirate.

Nevertheless the Committee believed La Follette and Taft to be the most appropriate choices under the terms of the resolution —particularly in view of the way in which they symbolized the progressive and conservative points of view on the great domestic issue that confronted the Senate during this century: the proper role of governmental activity in the economic and social life of this country.

But both were more than symbols. "Fighting Bob" La Follette, a great governor of Wisconsin whose influence is still felt in that state, was the outstanding Progressive of his day; and his struggle strongly influenced the economic reforms of the Wilson and Roosevelt eras. Professor Henry S. Commager thought him "an obvious choice for the period around the turn of the century. . . . A man who did more to bring about Progressivism than anyone who was in the Senate in his generation." An outstanding political scientist who also picked La Follette over the other great Progressives of this century, Dr. E. E. Schattschneider of Wesleyan, called La Follette "the most vigorous and important exponent of liberal Republicanism in the Senate in the first quarter of the twentieth century." However isolated he may have been in the Senate, and however short-sighted his views on foreign policy may seem to most of us, his impressive legislative accomplishments which are outlined in the Committee Report, his tireless battles to make government serve all the people, and his deeply felt insight into social and economic forces, all combined to shape a career we rightfully honor today.

Bob Taft was also more than a symbol. All of us here who served with him would agree, even though on many occasions we may have disagreed with him, that he was a figure of many dimensions. His name offers logical balance to the name of La Follette in our group of five, just as he himself offered logical balance during the days when the role of the opposition was more difficult. The distinguished historian Alpheus T. Mason of Princeton ranked Taft with the Great Triumvirate of Clay, Calhoun and Webster because he "succeeded in being a strong party man without being blinded by partisan considerations." Quincy Wright, along with other well-known professors including Clinton Rossiter of Cornell, pointed out in his letter that Taft's leadership of the conservative movement was all the greater because his "conservatism was qualified by his capacity to perceive necessary reforms." The fact that he was the leading choice among members of the Senate today is not without significance.

Nevertheless, because of the controversy still surrounding the names of Taft and La Follette, it is important to recall that Clay, Calhoun and Webster in their own times did not always enjoy the wide recognition of their talents that posterity has given them. Listen, for example, to these words spoken about Henry Clay: "He prefers the specious to the solid, and the plausible to the true. . . . He is a bad man, an impostor, a creator of wicked schemes." Those words were spoken by John C. Calhoun, who ridiculed Clay's lack of education, moral conduct and short temper. Daniel Webster said Clay was "his inferior in many respects"; and Andrew Jackson once characterized him as being as "reckless and as full of fury as a drunken man in a brothel." On the other hand, who was it that said that John C. Calhoun was a rigid, fanatic, ambitious, selfishly partisan and sectional "turncoat," with "too much genius and too little common sense," who would either die a traitor or a madman? Henry Clay, of course. When Calhoun boasted in debate that he had been Clay's political master, Clay retorted: "Sir, I would not own him as a slave." Both Clay and Calhoun from time to time fought with Webster; and from the other House, the articulate John Quincy Adams viewed with alarm "the gigantic intellect, the envious temper, the ravenous ambition and the rotten heart of Daniel Webster."

And yet our Committee has selected Henry Clay, Daniel Webster and John C. Calhoun—and felt it had no other choice. For over thirty years they dominated the Congress and the country, providing leadership and articulation on all the great issues of the growing nation—the tariff, fiscal policies, foreign relations, defense, internal improvements, agriculture, industrial development, westward expansion, states' rights and slavery. From time to time they supported and opposed each other for the presidency that each desired but never achieved. And despite whatever bitter words passed between them, their mutual respect for each other remained high. "I don't like Henry Clay," said John Calhoun, "I wouldn't speak to him, but, by God, I love him." Webster considered Calhoun "much the ablest man in the Senate. . . . He could have demolished Newton, Calvin or even John Locke as a logician. . . . Whatever his aspirations, they were high, honorable and noble. . . . There was nothing groveling or low or nearly selfish that came near the head or the heart of Mr. Calhoun." Henry Clay predicted that Calhoun's principles would "descend to posterity under the sanction of a great name." And whatever John Quincy Adams may have thought of Webster's "rotten heart," he considered his celebrated reply to Hayne to be the "most significant [act] since the founding of the Constitution."

This is not to say that objections cannot be raised to each of the three. Criticisms of Henry Clay's moral conduct, scholarship and political schemes may well be justified; and there are those who feel he carried the principle of compromise too far. It is true that Clay said "It is a rule with me, when acting either in a public or a private character, to attempt nothing more than what there exists a prospect of accomplishment." And yet his spirit of compromise, in the words of Carl Schurz, "was illumined by a grand conception of the destinies of his country, a glowing national spirit, a lofty patriotism." His greatest anxiety was the preservation of the Union; and few did more to contribute toward its salvation. Abraham Lincoln called the Great Pacificator "my beau ideal of a statesman, the man for whom I fought all my humble life." An extraordinarily gifted figure, his brilliant oratorical talents, unusual vitality and a unique gift of winning the hearts as well as the minds of his countrymen all enabled his three great compromise proposals in 1820, 1833 and 1850 to save the Union until it grew strong enough to save itself. "No other American politician," as Vernon Parrington has observed, "has been so loved by a hero-worshiping electorate—and so lovable."

Daniel Webster, it is true, portrayed, in the words of one of his intimate friends, an extraordinary "compound of strength and weakness, dust and divinity." It is true that he accepted a retainer from Nicholas Biddle of the Bank of the United States; that he accepted favors from the New England manufacturers; and that his decisions both as a senator and as a secretary of state appear to have been open to improper influence. Yet there is no serious evidence that his views on the Bank, the tariff and foreign policy would have been any different without these dubious connections—and on the contrary Professor Allan Nevins has written that he demonstrated more than any other colleague real insight into the problems of public finance, moderate protectionism and international affairs. Whatever may have been petty about his financial affairs, there was nothing petty about his moral stature in times of national crisis or in his dedication to the Union.

No list of outstanding senators would be regarded as complete without Webster. Professor Commager wrote the Committee that "Webster is so obvious a choice that it would be superfluous to attempt a justification. Indeed if a single name were to be selected, that name would be, almost by common consent, Webster." And in 1900 when balloting began for the American Hall of Fame at New York University, Webster was tied with Abraham Lincoln for second place immediately behind George Washington. Many members of our panel of scholars stated that they selected Webster for the permanent impression left by his constitutional ideas despite his faults of character. My old government professor at Harvard, Arthur N. Holcombe, wrote me: "Though a blot on his record, these dealings were not so far out of line with the political morals of his time as they would be today. Allowance should be made for the lower standard of political ethics at the senatorial level then."

The same answer, I believe, can be given to those objecting to the views entertained and defended by John C. Calhoun. "He was wrong," Pulitzer Prize-winning historian Arthur Schlesinger, Jr., wrote us, "but he was a greater man and senator than many people who have been right." In defending the views of his state and section on the practice of slavery, abhorrent to all of us today but a constitutionally recognized practice in his time, Calhoun was yielding neither to the pressures of expediency or immorality—nor did his opponents at the time so regard it. Calhoun was not a proponent of disunion—though he warned at the end of his career that secession might be the South's only means of achieving justice, he fought long and hard to keep the South in the Union.

Generally judged to be the most notable political thinker ever to sit in the Senate, whose doctrine of concurrent majorities has permanently influenced our political theory and practice, John Calhoun did more than any other senator in the nineteenth century, in the words of Professor Nevins, "to make men think clearly and carefully on fundamental political questions. . . . He was a model member in the purity of his public and private life, in his incessant industry and in his efforts to master completely the main issues of his day."

And thus I am among those who would regard it as inconceivable not to name Clay, Webster and Calhoun on the list of five outstanding senators. No other senators have ever rivaled the unparalleled leadership and statesmanship which they gave to a growing and anxious nation during a critical era when the Senate was the nation's most important body. Whatever objections may be raised to their views and morals, in my opinion, must be balanced against their achievements—and against the high-mindedness and dignity which moved them at their finest moments.

As I have pointed out in the Committee report, which outlines their careers and achievements in more detail, the objections which can be raised to each of the five names selected—just as they can be raised against any name suggested—are outweighed in the case of these five senators by their over-all statesmanship, their service to the nation, and their impact on the Senate, the country, and our history. They are not necessarily, as already pointed out, the five greatest senators; nor are they necessarily the most blameless or irreproachable ones, nor models of contemporary behavior. Allowance must be made of the times, the morals, and the practices of the period in which each served; and political and policy differences should not diminish their claim to the label "outstanding."

Obviously everyone will not agree. The distinguished Yale professor, Samuel Flagg Bemis, who nominated Webster even though one of his books has been cited as an authority for Webster's laxity in financial matters, told me of an interesting precedent in this matter of portraits (a precedent which went the other way)—namely, that when the Bemis book appeared, the large portrait of Webster which balanced that of John Hay suddenly and mysteriously disappeared from the anteroom of the Secretary of State in Washington, apparently relegated to a more obscure hanging in some other room. Senators, too, will disagree; and in filing this report with the Senate, I want to make clear my hope that senators who do disagree with our conclusions will voice their objections or preferences to the Senate. Should a majority be opposed to the recommendations contained in our report, I assume under the parliamentary situation it would be possible for the Senate to reject it. Although individual senators were asked to submit nominations, no attempt was made to clear our findings with senators from the same home states as those proposed—and the Committee will be glad to defend its choices against whatever objections may be raised.

There is always much for which a chairman is grateful in filing a report. I am grateful for the kindness and cooperation of my four colleagues on the Committee—Senators Bridges, Russell, Bricker and Mansfield—who brought to this task the wisdom and sense of responsibility it deserved. I am grateful to the distinguished historian Allan Nevins, who graciously consented to serve as chairman of our Historical Advisory Committee, and whose counsel was of particular value to me; and to all the members of our panel of scholars who responded to our inquiry with thoughtful, helpful letters. I am particularly delighted to be able to report that the Committee spent less than 6 per cent of its budget! Of the $10,000 allotted to the Committee under the resolution, $9,466.68 has been returned.

May I conclude by stressing once again that I believe this project to have had for this body considerable value beyond the basic necessity for its creation. The Senate emphasized in the discussion preceding passage of the resolution, and the Committee has attempted to emphasize during the past year, that there is considerable merit in stimulating interest among the general public and the Senate itself in the high traditions of the Senate, in the political problems faced by even our most distinguished statesmen, and in the high standards of the past which might be inspiring or emulated today. It is the Committee's hope that the considerable interest evoked by this project will be of value at a time when the democratic way of life is under pressure from without and the problems and conflicting pressures involved in the political profession are frequently misunderstood within our own country. The Committee has attempted in a small way to focus the nation's attention upon the Senate and its distinguished traditions, upon the high quality of men who have served in the Senate, and upon the significant role that the Senate has played in the history of our nation. The members of the Special Committee thus hope that an increasing awareness of national and senatorial history which should not be forgotten will be of benefit to the general public and to the Senate itself.

I wish at this time, Mr. President, to file our report with the Senate.

ECONOMIC POLICIES

ENEMIES WITHIN THE HOUSE OF LABOR [1]

James B. Carey [2]

James B. Carey, president of the International Union of Electrical, Radio and Machine Workers, AFL-CIO, and secretary treasurer of AFL-CIO Industrial Union Department, gave this address at the twentieth convention of the Pennsylvania Industrial Union Council, CIO, at Philadelphia, February 27, 1957.

The significance of this address lay in its strong voicing of the AFL-CIO's determination in establishing an Ethical Practices Code in February 1957. The consolidated organization was making a resolute effort to stamp out the "enemies within the house of labor"—labor racketeering, corrupt unionism, and "venal corruption," growing out of the "undeniable fact that the House of Labor has termites" and "therefore needs a fumigation."

Carey has established himself as a student of labor's philosophy; as an effective composer of speeches; and as an adroit speaker, both in prepared manuscript delivery and in extempore speaking on radio and television.

This speech was delivered in the midst of the 1957 labor activity to "clean house" and to offset the possible outcomes of the illegal use of labor funds and liaison between unions and racketeers.

On January 24, 1957, for example, the Executive Board of the International Union of Electrical, Radio and Machine Workers had adopted a Code of Ethical Practices.

The Senate Committee on Improper Activities in the Labor or Management Field (Senator John McClellan of Arkansas, chairman) began its investigations early in January and continued at intervals throughout the year. Dave Beck, president of the International Brotherhood of Teamsters, invoked the Fifth Amendment some eighty times on November 26 and 27, when summoned before the Committee and asked whether he had dipped into union funds for his private benefit. The AFL-CIO Executive Council on January 28 ordered its affiliates to oust any officials who invoked the Fifth Amendment on grounds of possible self-incrimination or who re-

---

[1] Text supplied by Les Finnegan, executive assistant to James B. Carey, president of the International Union of Electrical, Radio and Machine Workers, with the permission of the speaker for this reprint.

[2] For biographical note, see Appendix.

fused to answer questions concerning their alleged racketeering and illegal use of union funds.

On April 7, Walter Reuther and the United Automobile workers in their convention pledged cooperation with the Senate Committee in its investigation. The AFL-CIO on March 29 had suspended Beck as a council member and vice president, and on May 20 expelled him.

The International Brotherhood of Teamsters was suspended on October 24 by the Executive Council. At the December 1957 meeting in Atlantic City, New Jersey, by a five to one vote, the AFL-CIO expelled the Teamsters.

The Bakery and Confectionery Workers International Union of America was suspended on November 15 for "failure to and refusal to" meet a November 15 deadline to "eliminate corrupt influences from the Union."

The investigation led to the forced retirement of Dave Beck and to his indictment on charges of grand larceny. The hearings also produced evidence that linked James R. Hoffa, president-elect of the Teamsters, with New York gangsters and racketeers.

Such was the background of the Carey speech and the subsequent events related to these "enemies within the house of labor."

This, the twentieth and last regular convention of the Pennsylvania State CIO, is both a solemn and portentous occasion.

I am extremely proud of having had the opportunity of addressing both the first convention of the Pennsylvania State CIO and its last convention. And if, in this final convention, we are inclined a bit toward sentimentality that indulgence is not only justified but appropriate. We would be less than human and we would be unfeeling toward our own hectic history if we did not, during these two climatic days, glance backward over the long, long path we have traveled during the past two decades. It would be surprising if we didn't look back even with a touch of nostalgia to the excitements and turbulences of our early years.

Those years have already started to take on something of a rosy, romantic glow. It's an astonishing thing but today, looking back over the receding years, it somehow doesn't seem so terrible that we had our heads clobbered by Pearl Bergoff goon squads or took beatings efficiently administered by Pinkerton thugs. The pain somehow seems to have disappeared from our recollections of broken arms and legs handed out by Baldwin-Felts professional strikebreakers. Today we look back on bloody noses given us by Railway Audit detectives or by Chowderhead Cohen almost as the equivalent of a merit badge or a distinguished service medal.

One reason, I believe, for the slightly romantic glow with which we are beginning to surround those early years is the fact that we won and our enemies were defeated. True, we lost battles—that is to say, we lost strikes and lost organizing campaigns—but we won the war. We are here today, but the once-powerful union-busting outfits and labor spy rackets have fallen into unmourned oblivion.

This twentieth convention of the Pennsylvania State CIO demonstrates that labor in this state, as in others, continues to grow larger and stronger. But the once-feared Pearl Bergoff? He's now a footnote in the histories of labor. The Pinkerton thugs? They're now embalmed in the pages of the La Follette Committee Reports. The Baldwin-Felts strikebreakers? I understand there are one or two of them left in wax museums. The Railway Audit detectives and Chowderhead Cohen? They are lost in ancient history as completely as Herbert Hoover's high celluloid collars and belief in the divine right of millionaire robber barons.

Yes, the world has changed in the nearly twenty years since the Pennsylvania CIO was born, but it's not enough to say merely that. The world has changed because we changed the world. The upsurge of the American labor movement in the depths of the Great Depression became one of the greatest moral and ethical crusades in history, a crusade that authoritative historians have termed "a second American revolution."

We of the labor movement more than any other group changed the moral and ethical climate of our country. We made employers moral and made the government moral.

We made employers moral by compelling them to abandon their ancient dog-eat-dog economic philosophy and forcing them to accept the fact that labor is not a commodity but a grouping of individual human beings with the same rights, privileges and capacities as employers. We made employers moral by compelling them to understand that their responsibilities did not begin and end with profits but that they had inescapable social and economic obligations to the workers who created their wealth, their leisure and their luxuries.

We made the government moral by helping elect an administration responsive to the needs of the people and by erasing forever the concept of government as an instrument in the service of big business and industry. We made the government moral by insisting successfully, for the first time in history, that government has a responsibility to alleviate the mass unemployment, hunger and homelessness created by the free enterprise system. We made government moral by establishing its obligation to bring humanity and decency to the cut-throat economic jungle created by big business and industry We made government moral by demonstrating that it had both the right and the duty to intervene in the prescription of minimum wages, maximum hours, healthful working conditions, the prohibition of child labor, the right to bargain collectively, old age security, and a host of other benefits and protections.

Pennsylvania was the birthplace of the CIO; therefore, it must be counted as the birthplace of the moral and ethical crusade that became the "second American revolution." Your organization, therefore, has special reason for pride. When the CIO held its first constitutional convention in Pittsburgh in November 1938 your Pennsylvania Industrial Union Council was its host. In addition, Pennsylvania achieved the first successful unionization of such industries as mining, electrical, radio and machine manufacturing, and steel.

If we are investing those early years of the CIO with something of a romantic aura we may also be starting to forget the enormity of the strides we made in those early days.

For example, next Saturday, March 2, will be the twentieth anniversary of the signing of the first contract between the United Steelworkers of America and the United States Steel Corporation.

That first contract was a revolution in steel. Among other things, it jumped the pay rate for common laborers to 62.5 cents an hour. The significance of this lies in the fact that during the previous thirty-seven years—from 1900 to 1937—the rate for common laborers had increased only 15 cents, up to 47 cents an hour in 1937.

No wonder, therefore, that one of my sharpest recollections of that First Pennsylvania CIO Convention nearly twenty years ago is that we were people in a terrible hurry back in 1938. We were in a hurry to change the face of the American labor movement and in a hurry to change the world we were living in.

God knows the world we were living in did need changing and changing in a hurry One of the resolutions passed by that historic first convention pointed out that there were at that time 13 million American workers unemployed. The American economy in 1938 was only slowly dragging itself out of the most devastating and degrading depression in history; mass unemployment, homelessness and hunger still stalked the richest land on earth.

It's a fascinating fact that today, almost twenty years later, most of the moral and ethical issues that occupied your first convention are still moral and ethical issues for American workers in 1957. To mention just a few of them:

Improved unemployment compensation; expanded social security; better minimum wage legislation; a national housing program; an equitable Federal labor law; and effective civil rights statutes.

I said these were moral and ethical issues, and indeed they are. They involve economic and social morality and such ethical concepts as justice, decent living standards and human dignity. They are moral and ethical issues, moreover, because they affect not simply trade union members but all the nation's wage earners, the economic health of their communities and the economic health of the nation as a whole.

I want to suggest that your forthcoming creation of a great, new, unified labor movement in Pennsylvania should be the occasion for a fresh evaluation of the moral and ethical responsibilities both of trade unionism and of business and industry.

Such a reappraisal is vital for two reasons:

First, the essential purposes of establishing a new, unified trade union movement are moral and ethical insofar as we seek to create a more effective instrument in the service of human welfare and social good. Second, a reappraisal of business ethics and morality may disclose whether unionism and business share, to any degree, common ethical and moral objectives.

Turning first, therefore, to trade unionism, let me put the problem to you—as I see it—as frankly and as bluntly as I possibly can.

The American labor movement today is faced with a moral and ethical problem as crucially important as the problem that produced the CIO and the "second American revolution" in the mid-1930's.

Very possibly it is an even bigger problem, because this one has arisen not outside the labor movement but from within. This is a problem—a crisis, if you wish—that has emerged not from any external situation, not from defects in our economy, not from union-hating employers, not from antilabor legislation.

On the contrary, this problem, this crisis, has been generated almost entirely from within the labor movement. We cannot, justifiably, blame others. Whatever eventuates—for good or for evil—the labor movement must accept the responsibility.

The cancer of labor racketeering, of corrupt unionism, menaces not only the good name, the prestige and reputation of the labor movement today; it also threatens the very future of our development as a free labor movement.

By itself labor racketeering is immoral and unethical. But it may also have three other direct effects.

First, labor racketeering—no matter how limited—smears all labor with the foul taint of corruption.

Second, labor racketeering places incomparable propaganda weapons in the hands of union-hating employers to render organizing work either impossible or enormously more difficult.

Third, labor racketeering provides the excuse and justification for savagely repressive antilabor laws in Congress and state legislatures.

But here let us make one thing extremely clear. We do not and cannot confine our definition of union corruption to statutory crimes, to indictable offenses. Corruption is not demarcated by such felonies as bribery, extortion, theft of union funds, shakedowns of employers, financial alliances with the underworld of gambling and vice, or kickbacks from the investment of welfare and pension funds.

There is such a thing as venal corruption. There can be crimes in the labor movement that are not illegal but morally reprehensible.

Venal corruption, I think, can arise when union officials are men who view their organizations not as a sacred trust, not as a brotherhood, not as the preliminary realization of an ideal, but rather as a business enterprise, a cold-blooded commercial undertaking.

Venal corruption can arise when enormous gaps develop between the living standards of union members and the living standards of union leaders, when union officers start to own large business enterprises, apartment houses, stables of race horses.

Venal corruption can arise when union officials come—consciously or unconsciously—to think of the labor movement as a means to personal enrichment, huge bank accounts, swimming pools in their front yards and artificial waterfalls in their living rooms.

Those who, either legally or illegally, use unionism solely as a means to personal enrichment deserve to be hounded out of the American labor movement as fast, as furiously and as finally as we can find the means to do it!

Such men are not unionists, but antiunionists! They are not labor, but antilabor! They are more dangerous to the democratic labor movement than the worst of union-hating managements! They are more poisonous than professional spies and strikebreakers! They are more destructive than the union-busting goon squads of two decades ago! They are more contaminating than any kind of decay that can afflict a labor union!

Because they betray us and our ideals from within the labor movement, they are doubly abominable and doubly dangerous. Because they exploit the sanctuary of union brotherhood to despoil the very name and idea of brotherhood, they bring a loathsome contagion into our midst.

We can fight reactionary employers and we can hold our own in combat wth union-hating managements because we know pretty thoroughly where they stand. They don't pretend to be the opposite of what they are. They don't (at least not often these days) attempt to betray our organizations from within. Our fighting with management in recent years has become increasingly above-board. We know who our enemies are in the arena of economic conflict.

But we're not so sure today that we know who our enemies are within the labor movement. We know, however, that they are there, using the labor movement as a shield for their despicable practices. We know that trade unionism has been and is still perverted into a protective cover for criminal activities.

The undeniable fact is that the House of Labor has termites and, therefore, needs a fumigation!

There's no sense in trying to reassure ourselves with the fact that the number of termites is limited. We risk self-deception by repeating to ourselves that only a very small percentage of unions and workers are involved in racketeering.

But the fact of the matter is that we do not know today how far the termites have eaten into the foundations, nor actually how extensive the infestation is.

Of one thing we are certain, however. One single national union that is corrupt is one too many! One single local union that is run by racketeers is one too many!

Corruption anywhere in trade unionism is morally indefensible. Perhaps in only one other institution in contemporary society—our religious bodies—is there a greater obligation to moral purity than in the labor movement.

Business and industry are institutions erected frankly to the purpose of profit. They make little or no pretense of being either altruistic or humanitarian. Hence there is a minimum of hypocrisy when business and industry operate unethically or for immoral ends. The public has been conditioned to accept business immorality—and even business criminality—as an inevitable part of the dog-eat-dog world which business and the free enterprise system have created for themselves.

But there's no such immunity for organized labor, because labor professes to be an altruistic and humanitarian movement. More than that, we aspire to the highest moral and ethical ideals, and proclaim that our only motivations are brotherhood, economic justice, human dignity, and the national welfare.

Within such a spiritual framework as this, consequently, there can be no room for moral laxity or lapses from high principle.

More than any other organizations in our society, trade unions ought to be able to live inside out. They should be able to disclose themselves fully to public view, to scrutiny by friend and foe alike. More and more unions find it possible to do so. It is to be regretted that in other instances the complete disclosure of union finances and resources might very well become an open invitation to employers to risk a strike or undertake a decertification campaign.

Yes, it is true that only a very limited area of trade unionism —as far as we know—is affected by corruption, and only a small percentage of unions and workers are victimized by racketeering.

But that fact doesn't mean a thing to big business and industry. The truth is that every union represented in this convention is finding that new organizing has been made immeasurably tougher by the continuing disclosures of corruption and racketeering in the labor movement.

Organizing has become tougher because: (1) unorganized workers have read the newspaper stories and concluded that because one union or two unions are corrupt all unions must be, or (2) employers are actively exploiting the corruption disclosures as antiunion propaganda.

Either way I'm afraid that for thousands upon thousands of unorganized workers the tremendous accomplishments of organized labor over many decades can be obliterated by a few screaming headlines dealing with isolated cases of labor racketeering.

We cannot know, for example, but we can easily guess what psychological balance was achieved by two different occurrences here in Philadelphia last week.

One was the dedication of a splendid new $1.5 million union health and medical center, the realization of a longtime dream of twenty-eight Philadelphia unions. Here was a manifestation of union brotherhood, humanitarianism and social conscience at its best.

The headlines were fair; however, it was a one-shot news story for the local press.

But in one or more Philadelphia newspapers on that same day—and every day since, as far as I can ascertain—there has been another kind of headline and another kind of news story dealing with labor.

This running news story has recounted the sordid and sickening history of a flagrantly racket-controlled local union here in Philadelphia, a union run by criminals and ex-convicts for the sole purpose of defrauding workers out of tens of thousands of dollars while at the same time extorting additional thousands from their employers.

Here is one of the foulest stenches ever to afflict the city of Philadelphia where the American labor movement was born and where so much union history has been made.

Discussing as we are the question of union morality you will, I am sure, find particularly interesting the moral safeguards established by the constitution of this local union.

This, if it were not so tragic and vicious, could be comic. The ex-convicts, the goons who run this racket union, who offer kickbacks from members' dues to employers, who seek sweetheart and sell-out contracts, who employ coercion and terror on employees and employers alike, these men who represent virtually everything that is hateful to honest unionism, these creeps had the brazen effrontery to write a local union constitution which declares in Article 1—and get this!—"An applicant for membership must be of good moral character. . . ."

Which do you think has made the deeper and more permanent impression on the average, nonunion citizen of Philadelphia —the dedication of the wonderful new union health center or the disclosures of a rotten racket outfit masquerading as a labor union? Which will be remembered? Which will do most to shape and color public attitudes toward labor? I'm afraid we know only too well.

In the face of screaming outrages like this one are we to console ourselves with the recollection that, still and all, only a tiny portion of labor is involved? In the face of similar abominations dredged up by congressional investigating committees, are we to take refuge in percentages and in pious hope that such conditions will remedy themselves?

No, of course we can't. The labor movement has already waited far too long to cut out these festering sores. We are paying a heavy penalty already for allowing them to continue, and we are likely to pay even heavier penalties in the future.

Probably every union represented in this convention, as I remarked earlier, has had organizing made tougher by these revelations of union corruption. Antiunion employers from coast to coast and from Canada to the Gulf of Mexico have jumped gleefully on these disclosures ad now are using them as clubs with which to clobber union organizing campaigns.

Our IUE organizing campaigns, for example, have recently had to confront that type of propaganda weapon in the hands of huge corporations and small companies alike. The stories of union corruption are being hurled at us by officials of the billion-dollar General Electric and Westinghouse companies, among others.

To cite only one instance, the IUE is currently conducting a determined campaign to organize a new General Electric plant in Hendersonville, North Carolina. GE, it is clear, would like to brainwash its employees into believing that union dues are entirely devoted to providing union leaders with luxuries and the means for riotous living. The GE employee newspaper in Hendersonville reported in a recent issue, for example, that a congressional committee discovered that one union leader had:

used union funds to pay his personal bills; another official allegedly used money from the membership to finance his stable of race horses and pay for the upkeep of horse vans, and additional union money was used to buy and repair this same official's personal automobile.

And so it goes. GE hopes, of course, that some of the mud it flings will stick to the IUE, and that a majority of workers will associate the charges of misused union funds with our international union.

Make no mistake, we're going to have more of this kind of vicious propaganda thrown at us. Management likes it; management believes it works. I'm afraid that maybe it does; so are other union officials I've talked to.

There, then, is part of the picture of how employers can use—and do use—a few instances of union corruption to smear the entire labor movement.

But that doesn't end it. Those few instances have also put potent antiunion weapons into the hands of reactionaries in Congress and in state legislatures. Yesterday as the Senate Select Committee on Improper Activities in the Labor or Management Field opened hearings in Washington we learned for the first time that the investigation is now scheduled to continue for a full year. Its chairman has been quoted as saying, even before the hearings opened, that legislation is necessary because "working people must be protected from a form of extortion, theft and embezzlement. . . ."

In nearly a score of state legislatures new and more repressive antilabor laws are being prepared, more often than not at the instigation of industrial employers. And the excuse for these new laws will be, more than ever before, the disclosures of union corruption and racketeering.

The influential New York *Times*, for example, in an editorial on abuses in the administration of union welfare funds, first demanded that Congress pass legislation to outlaw these abuses, then added, "And state legislatures throughout the country should enact their own laws. . . ."

We can well imagine what kind of laws will be proposed in states that already have right-to-scab laws in operation, states that encourage municipalities to enact statutes requiring union organizers to buy licenses and pay daily fees for the right to organize.

Those are the penalties under which we're suffering today because we allowed a handful of racketeers and businessmen masquerading as unionists to continue their criminal careers inside the labor movement.

Let me emphasize right here that I have no intention nor desire to paint a picture that is entirely dark. On the contrary, there are dramatically bright aspects, features in which the labor movement can take pride.

We can, for example, ask ourselves: what other movement has set out voluntarily to eradicate the evil elements inside itself, even at the risk of weakening its organizational strength?

What other institution or major organization in American society has undertaken to police itself, to cleanse its own ranks of wrong-doing and wrong-doers?

What employer organization, such as the United States Chamber of Commerce or the National Association of Manufacturers would expel, suspend or even denounce an affiliated company found guilty of corruption or other crimes?

The extent to which trade unionism is determined to drive the termites from the house of labor was shown earlier this month when the AFL-CIO Executive Council, with only one dissenting vote, approved a set of Codes of Ethical Practices. In this unprecedented action, the AFL-CIO in effect declared war on corruption and racketeering. At long last the entire American labor movement was provided the means with which to free itself from corruption and the perversion of union ideals.

I am personally proud that a week before this announcement, the IUE adopted its own Code of Ethical Practices designed, as we declared, "to prohibit any conduct that would countenance racketeering, racism, corruption or undemocratic practices of any kind."

Our Code of Ethical Practices set new precedents as a comprehensive document, covering such areas of union operations as organizational work, administration of health-welfare-pension programs, the conduct of local union affairs including membership rights and elections, the management of local union funds, and enforcement.

Among other requirements, the IUE Code calls for strict financial accounting and control of union funds. In general it is intended "not only to promote the principles and practices of trade union democracy but also to encourage the expansion and diversification of democracy within our union."

The IUE, therefore, is determined to erect every possible barricade against the invasion of unethical practices or corruption. The adoption of similar codes of ethical practices by other unions, I feel, is inevitable.

Let me point out that both the AFL-CIO Codes of Ethical Practices and the IUE Code of Ethical Practices deal not only with illegal activities but also with activities that are simply unethical. Both Codes, therefore, seek not merely to penalize criminal actions but also to establish higher principles and standards of conduct for unions and union officials.

We have got to make these Codes of Ethical Practices work. They must be made to function swiftly and vigorously against corruption and racketeering wherever they are proved to exist.

The Codes can and should also be employed to eliminate the businessmen disguised as union leaders, or at the very least convert them into unionists. The Codes can and should have the effect of making union leadership more sensitive and more responsive to rank-and-file needs. They should help narrow whatever unreasonable gaps have grown up between the membership and leadership of unions.

The labor movement has delayed overlong the decisive action necessary to its renewal as a great moral and ethical crusade. The labor movement can make up for that lost time and for the indulgence of corruption in its ranks by hitting hard and fatally now at labor racketeering wherever it can be found.

We can redeem our mistakes and insure a healthy and accelerated growth for American trade unionism by not waiting for grand juries, state legislatures or congressional committees to do our work for us.

We can justify the vast trust placed in us by millions of American workers and prove worthy of the heritage of sacrifice and dedication bequeathed to us by the men and women of labor who have preceded us only if we guide this greatest of all free labor movements to new high levels of morality and integrity.

In that lies both the hope and the need of the labor movement's future; the need of our nation's future, also.

CIVIL RIGHTS LEGISLATION

FOR THE CIVIL RIGHTS BILL [1]

PAUL H. DOUGLAS [2]

Senator Paul H. Douglas (Democrat, Illinois) gave this speech on proposed civil rights legislation as part of his testimony before the Subcommittee on Constitutional Rights of the Senate Committee on the Judiciary, February 15, 1957.

During the months after his Judiciary Committee testimony, Senator Douglas continued to speak as a leading proponent of civil rights legislation. On April 18, for example, he gave the Senate a complete brief of his argument for such a bill. On June 9, he engaged in a long running debate reviewing every important phase of the problem.

In that debate, in reply to the contention of Senator Samuel J. Ervin (Democrat, North Carolina) that the bill should guarantee jury trials in contempt cases arising out of civil rights injunctions, Senator Douglas argued that Southern jurors would convict few or no white men for offenses against Negroes. Only qualified voters are allowed to serve on juries in most Southern states. Most southern Negroes are prevented from voting by the poll tax and other vote-preventing devices. An amendment to require jury trials in such cases of violation of civil rights, Douglas argued, would "nullify the right-to-vote provisions of that bill in direct proportion to the discriminations against voting that now exist."

The House of Representatives, after six days of debate, passed the civil rights bill on June 18. The Senate, after the Judiciary Committee with Senator James O. Eastland of Mississippi, chairman, had failed to act, placed the House bill on the Senate calendar, on June 20.

The Senate bill, embodying President Eisenhower's program, was composed of four parts: Part I called for the creation of a Civil Rights Commission to study the situation and make recommendations for further action by Congress. Part II provided for a new Assistant Attorney General in the civil rights area. Part III authorized the Attorney General to seek court injunctions in cases constituting a threat to civil rights.

---

[1] From report of proceedings of the Subcommittee on Constitutional Rights of the Senate Committee on the Judiciary, February 15, 1957. See the *Hearings Before the Subcommittee on Constitutional Rights of the Committee on the Judiciary, United States Senate, 85th Congress, first Session, February 14 to March 5, 1957,* p 100-21.

[2] For biographical note, see Appendix.

Part IV authorized the Attorney General specifically to obtain injunctions against violators of civil rights. Federal judges were authorized to rule against violators on contempt charges without a jury.

The Senate floor debate began on July 16. Northern Democrat Senator Joseph O'Mahoney, of Wyoming, offered and supported a modified jury trial amendment to the bill. Senator Douglas and some colleagues held out strongly for a non-jury trial bill. Against any bill at all were diehard Southerners. They nevertheless with effective strategy worked to water down the bill as much as possible. For arguments in the Senate, pro and con, after July 16, see the speeches of Senators Samuel Ervin and Wayne Morse and the introductions to these speeches.[3]

In this prolonged debate on civil rights in the United States Senate during July 1957, one of the most brilliant debates in that body in the twentieth century, Senator Douglas, like Senators Wayne Morse, Samuel Ervin, Jacob Javits, and Richard Russell, demonstrated repeatedly his accurate and logical arguments, worthy of the best senatorial traditions.[4]

With the assurances given by the leadership of both parties in the Senate, with the support of the Administration expressed by the President and by the Attorney General, and with the backing of the great majority of the American people, perhaps we can begin to hope that the stalemate on civil rights in Congress will be ended.

You have it within your power to take the first essential step in a new advance toward human freedom.

Any review of the past half-century reveals many gains in equality of opportunity. These have resulted from both voluntary and governmental action. Court decisions going back nearly forty years and culminating in the school cases have opened many doors. Administrative actions under Presidents Roosevelt, Truman and Eisenhower have likewise eliminated many discriminations.

But, since the enactment of the Fourteenth and Fifteenth Amendments to the Constitution and the civil rights laws of the Reconstruction Period, the direct gains by Federal legislation have been nil.

Congress has not kept pace with the courts—or the Executive—or the people. Neither has it measured up to the needs.

[3] See below, p 116-27.
[4] For further comment on Douglas as a speaker, see *Representative American*
[3] See below, p 116-27.

Despite significant—and often heart-warming—gains, there is no question that denials of equal opportunity are still many and grievous. We find them in employment, in education, in transportation, in housing, in health facilities, in public recreation, in the right to vote, and even in our courts.

These denials are not limited to any one section of the country. In varying degrees and in varying forms, they are nation-wide. The record of the hearings before Senate and House committees—and, indeed, the daily press—is full of the evidence of our failures in these matters.

This form of man's inhumanity to man, wherever it occurs in our nation, violates one of the fundamental principles of our democracy, namely, that men are to be judged on their individual merits, not according to the accident of their membership in one race or another, or by their choice of a religious affiliation. It offends the American sense of fair play and breaches our basic religious and political teachings that "God hath made of one blood all nations of men," and that "all men are created equal and are endowed by their Creator with certain unalienable rights."

It is also clear today that these denials of our constitutional and religious principles adversely affect the struggle of freedom against tyranny in the world. With the Communists reaching out to the uncommitted people of the Middle East and Africa and Southeast Asia, each housing riot in Illinois, each school riot in Kentucky, and each bombing of a pastor's home or intimidation of a would-be Negro voter in Alabama or Mississippi becomes not only an affront to human dignity here in this country, but a defeat for freedom in its tough world struggle for survival.

The voluntary processes that slowly change men's hearts, the local and state laws and Federal judicial and executive action that have advanced men's rights and yet fallen so short of the goal of equal opportunity, therefore, need the new impetus and backing of Congressional action. And the time for action is long overdue.

Of the various worthy proposals before you, the most fundamental in my view is that which would strengthen the protections of the right to vote. This right is denied not only by the poll tax in five states, but even more flagrantly by open and covert intimidation in numerous others. The record of discriminatory administration of voter qualification tests, of economic pressures and bodily threats to prevent persons from voting and of systematic purging of large groups from voter lists is a long one. . . .

Yet, if we can help to restore and maintain this right to vote, many of the other present discriminations practiced against Negroes, Indians and Mexican-Americans will be self-correcting. For once these citizens have the effective right to vote, they will have political power. Public office holders will then have to take their needs and wishes into account, and these citizens will be able to redress their just grievances by constitutional means and within the framework of the democratic process. . . .

This protection of the right to political participation is, therefore, a vital key to many other rights.

It seems to me wise to cover primaries in the elections protected by the criminal provisions of the law. I am particularly impressed by the provisions permitting the Attorney General to proceed in Federal courts for preventive relief by suits for injunctions. Punishment after the event is never a solution for a denial of rights. Preventive action before the denial is complete may actually preserve the right that would otherwise be lost. . . .

Mr. Chairman, the logic of a Commission on Civil Rights to give us greater knowledge and understanding of these complex problems, of a special division in the Department of Justice to give greater attention to the enforcement of existing laws, of broader powers to move for injunctive relief against various violations of civil rights, seems to me too clear to require elaboration. If elaboration is desired, the hearings back for twenty or more years on some of these subjects will provide it. . . .

Once this bill is before the Senate at a reasonably early date, with all the support that has been promised, we shall hope to be able to surmount the obstacle that hitherto has blocked the passage of such legislation, the eternal filibuster.

If all of those who have said—contrary to my belief—that the present Senate rules permit the passage of a meaningful civil rights bill will vote for it and for cloture, after a proper debate, perhaps it may yet succeed. No one will be happier than I to have it proved that the Senate, under its present rules, is *not* the graveyard of civil rights.

It is up to this Committee first and to all of us in the Senate, then, to determine whether we shall merely reflect the conflicts and failures of our society on these important issues of human freedom—or represent in our affirmative action, the best hopes and ideals of our nation for equality of opportunity.

AGAINST THE RIGHTS BILL [5]

SAMUEL J. ERVIN, JR. [6]

Senator Samuel J. Ervin, Jr. (Democrat, North Carolina) opened the Senate debate on the civil rights issue on July 8, 1957.

The North Carolina Senator led the Southern attack on the bill by a new Southern strategy. Instead of denouncing the whole idea of civil rights legislation, he and his Southern strategists focused their thunder on specific weaknesses of the pending bill.

Senator Ervin, formerly a North Carolina Supreme Court Judge, developed logical and intricate arguments to amend the legislation in general and especially to support a trial-by-jury provision. Senator Richard B. Russell of Georgia, also legally well trained and experienced as a constitutional expert, helped with the argument.

The first attack by these Southern strategists was on Part III of the bill. They argued that it would give the Federal Government unprecedented powers to force the Northern view of civil rights on the South. Part III, they argued, was entirely too broad (e.g., it would include segregation in the schools). Their argument, convincing to the moderates, led to the passage of amendments as proposed by moderates Clinton P. Anderson (Democrat, New Mexico), and George D. Aiken (Republican, Vermont). Thus the heart and operative section of Part III was removed and the issue was limited to voting rights.

For this Southern success Senator Ervin was largely responsible. Ervin's legal and constitutional arguments then focused on the "weaknesses" of Part IV, which gave the Attorney General authority to serve court injunctions against Southern officials who might interfere with Negro voting rights.

Any acceptable bill, argued Ervin and his colleagues, must provide for jury trial of officials cited for contempt of court under Part IV. Thus according to the Northern position, one civil right (to vote) would be guaranteed at the expense of another basic right (the right to a jury trial).

Although constitutionally and legally Ervin was not entirely on solid ground, his basic arguments and judicial interpretations had sufficient foundation to gain support from some senators who were discriminating interpreters of the entire issue relating to the area of decisions by judges and the area in which juries should be required.

For other arguments in this case and for the final outcome, see the speech below of Senator Wayne Morse, and the introduction to the speech.

[5] Text from the *Congressional Record*. 103:9904-15. July 8, 1957 (daily edition). Because of the length of this debate only a selection is here included.

[6] For biographical note, see Appendix.

The civil rights bill is certainly a deviation from the regular course. It is so conceived and so worded as to conceal rather than reveal its provisions and implications. Consequently, no one can obtain any reliable notion as to the significance of the legal quirks in the bill simply by reading it. To do this, one must spend weeks studying constitutional and legal history, legal rules, equitable principles, congressional enactments, and court decisions.

When one studies the civil rights bill in the light of these things, he discovers that its provisions and implications are utterly repugnant to the American constitutional and legal systems.

I oppose the civil rights bill. My opposition to it does not arise out of any matter of race. As a member of the school board in my home town and as a representative from my county in the North Carolina legislature, I have always done everything within my power to secure adequate educational opportunity for all of North Carolina's children of all races. As a lawyer, legislator, and judge, I have always done everything within my power to make it certain that all men stand equal before the law. As a private citizen and public official, I have always maintained that all qualified citizens of all races are entitled to vote.

I oppose the civil rights bill simply because I love our constitutional and legal systems, and desire above all things to preserve them for the benefit of all Americans of all races and all generations.

I know from my study of the civil rights bill that this will not be done if the bill or any substantial provisions in it are enacted into law. Diligent efforts are made to present the bill in the guise of a meritorious and mild bill.

It is said, for example, that the bill is simply designed to secure voting rights for Negroes in Southern states. I am going to say this bluntly, and I will say it plainly, so that he who runs may read and not err in so doing: There is not a scintilla of truth in the oft-repeated assertion that the bill is simply designed to secure voting rights to Negroes in Southern states. The bill proposes to confer upon the Attorney General of the United States the power to bring suit to suppress any of the practices specified in section 1985, title 42, of the United States Code. This section contains three subsections, and each of these subsections has many clauses. I call attention to one clause alone. It contains a provision authorizing the Attorney General to bring suit at the expense of the taxpayers in the name of the United States in cases where there are any conspiracies threatening or consummated to deprive any person of the equal protection of the law under the Fourteenth Amendment.

Under that clause alone the Attorney General can bring suit in behalf of any citizens of any race, any aliens of any race, and any private corporations within the territorial jurisdiction of the United States upon the allegation that they have been discriminated against by any statute of any state law or any application of state law to them on the part of any state or local officials. When we consider the fact that the term "state law" includes ordinances of municipalities, we get some idea of the breadth of the power which the Attorney General would have under this one clause. . . .

If one is to understand the laws and institutions of today, he must know the events of yesterday which gave them birth. For this reason, I deem it necessary to consider the origins of relevant constitutional and legal safeguards.

The founders of our government were wise men.

They knew that tyranny uses the forms of law to crush those who oppose her will.

They knew that the right of trial by jury is the best security of the people against governmental oppression.

They knew that the surest test of a witness is had when he is confronted on cross-examination by counsel for the adverse party.

They knew the history of the long struggle of the English people to secure and preserve such basic legal safeguards as the right of trial by jury and the right to confront and cross-examine adverse witnesses.

They knew the history of the repeated efforts of tyrannical kings and subservient parliaments to deprive the English people of the benefit of such legal safeguards.

They knew the history of the Court of Star Chamber, and rightly deduced from it "that the rights and liberties of the people will not long survive in any country where the administration of the law is committed exclusively to a caste endowed with boundless discretion and a long term of office, no matter how learned, able, and honest its members may be."

They knew the history of Chief Justice Jeffreys and his Bloody Assizes, and rightly inferred from it that tyranny on the bench is as objectionable as tyranny on the throne.

They knew that it is abhorrent to justice to punish any man twice for the same offense.

They knew that in 1764 and 1765 the British Parliament, at the instigation of King George III and his ministers, enacted the Sugar Act, the Stamp Act, and other measures, whereby they deprived American colonists of the right of trial by jury in cases arising under the revenue and trade laws by a device astoundingly similar to that invoked by the civil-rights bill, namely, "by extending beyond its ancient limits the jurisdiction of the courts of admiralty" in which trial by jury was not available.

They knew that the Stamp Act Congress, which was attended by delegates from nine of the thirteen colonies, forthwith met in New York, and adopted the Colonial Declaration of Rights of October 19, 1765, condemning this action of Parliament on the ground "that trial by jury is the inherent and invaluable right of every British subject in these Colonies."

They knew that in 1768 the British Parliament, at the urging of King George III and his ministers, enacted the statute known as 8 George III, chapter 22, whereby they deprived American colonists of the right of trial by jury in cases arising under the laws relating to trade and revenue by a repetition of the device resembling that invoked by the civil-rights bill, namely, "by extending beyond their ancient limits the powers of the courts of admiralty" in which trial by jury was not available.

They knew that the First Continental Congress adopted the Declaration of October 14, 1774, denouncing this action of the British Parliament on the ground that American colonists were entitled to the common law of England, and more especially to the great and inestimable privilege of being tried by their peers of the vicinage according to the course of that law.

They knew that the Declaration of Independence assigned the fact that American colonists had been deprived in many cases of the benefits of trial by jury as one of the injuries and usurpations requiring the American colonists to dissolve their political bonds with England.

They knew that tranquillity was not to be always anticipated in a republic; that strife would rise between classes and sections, and even civil war might come; and that in such times judges themselves might not be safely trusted in criminal cases, especially in prosecutions for political offenses, where the whole power of the executive is arrayed against the accused party.

They knew that what was done in the past might be attempted in the future, and that troublous times would arise, when rulers and people would become restive under restraint, and seek by sharp and decisive methods to accomplish ends deemed just and proper and that the principles of constitutional liberty would be in peril, unless established by irrepealable law.

They knew that the best part of the inheritance of America from England was the right of trial by jury, both in criminal cases and in suits at common law. For these reasons, the founders of our government enshrined these guarantees in the Constitution:

That "the trial of all crimes, except in cases of impeachment, shall be by jury"—Article III, section 2.

That "no person shall be held to answer for a capital, or otherwise infamous offense, unless on a presentment or indictment of a grand jury, except in cases arising in the land or naval forces, or in the militia, when in actual service in time of war or public danger; nor shall any person be subject for the same offense to be twice put in jeopardy of life or limb"—Amendment 5.

That "in all criminal prosecutions, the accused shall enjoy the right to a speedy and public trial, by an impartial jury of the State and district wherein the crime shall have been committed . . . and to be informed of the nature and cause of the accusation; to be confronted with the witnesses against him; to have compulsory process for obtaining witnesses in his favor, and to have the assistance of counsel for his defense"—Amendment 6.

That "in suits at common law, where the value in controversy shall exceed $20, the right of trial by jury shall be preserved"—Amendment 7. . . .

Mr. President, the civil rights bill is deliberately designed to confer upon the Attorney General of the United States the autocratic power to rob state and local officials and other Americans involved in civil rights disputes of these basic and invaluable safeguards created by the Founding Fathers and Congress to protect all Americans from bureaucratic and judicial tyranny, namely: The constitutional right of indictment by grand jury; the constitutional right of trial by petit jury; the constitutional right not to be twice put in jeopardy for the same offense; the statutory right of trial by jury in indirect contempt cases; and the statutory right to the benefit of limited punishment in indirect contempt cases.

CIVIL RIGHTS AND TRIAL BY JURY [7]

WAYNE L. MORSE [8]

Senator Wayne L. Morse (Democrat, Oregon) began his powerful Senate debate on the civil rights bill, on Tuesday, July 23, and completed it on Friday, July 26. The excerpt reprinted here is from the closing section of his speech of July 26.

During his two days of argument Senator Morse concentrated on the issue of the use of jury trials in cases arising out of civil rights injunctions.

The Southern argument, as we have noted in the introductions to the speeches above by Ervin and Douglas, was that civil contempt citations by judges alone against persons disobeying the court's injunction under the new bill would mean the "abolition of trial by jury." Eighteen Southern senators and some Northern supporters, headed by Senator Joseph O'Mahoney, agreed that the bill without an amendment to give such protection of trial by jury would be a tragic miscarriage of justice. The exclusive citation by the judges would protect the rights of one group by a process that would deny "a liberty equally precious—that of trial by jury."

Senator Morse again on August 1 spoke at length against the amendment.[9] But the Senate voted 51 to 42 to incorporate the O'Mahoney-Kefauver-Church amendment for jury trials in certain contempt cases.

On August 29 the Senate passed, 60 to 15, the act as compromised with the House version. The trial by jury issue was settled by a provision that a Federal judge could deny jury trial to persons accused of criminal contempt for alleged violation of right-to-vote injunctions. In such case the convicted person, if fined more than $300 or sentenced to more than forty-five days of imprisonment, could demand a trial by jury.

Despite this weakened version of the original bill the legislation was held to be a substantial gain in civil rights. Southern leaders for the first time "agreed to secure and protect by Federal intervention the civil rights of qualified Negroes to vote."

During 1957 Senator Morse continued to demonstrate his superior skill in debate and public speaking—both in the Senate and over the nation. His logical analysis of issues, especially the prolonged civil rights

[7] Text from the *Congressional Record*. 103:11599-605. July 23-26, 1957 (daily edition).

[8] For biographical note, see Appendix.

[9] See *Congressional Record*. 103:12137-9. August 1, 1957 (daily edition).

problems, reflected his wide legal background and his lively platform communicativeness. He was one of the four or five most effective Senate speakers of these months.[10]

In a law-abiding society failures and refusals to abide by court decrees are rare. They are rare because the lawful and orderly fashion of challenging the judgments and orders of Federal district courts, or any trial courts, is to appeal. Such an appeal can be based on the law, the factual record, or both. It has yet to be contended on this record that appellate courts will be anything but fair and judicial in reviewing judgments and orders.

What then is the issue? The issue is how alleged failures to comply with orders not appealed are to be tried. If we assume that defendants in these cases will be law abiding in the main, we are concerned with but a handful of cases. Indeed, if the history of our legal system is any guide, such cases will be the rare exception.

Or are we being told implicitly that there will be massive resistance to Federal court judgment and orders and that defendants will in the main take the law into their own hands? If this is the argument, what is our response? Are we being asked, in effect, to cripple or hobble the Federal district courts in the administration of this bill? Is the implicit argument that there will be hundreds of contempt actions because most defendants will defy the courts? And are we being told, in effect, that because we can expect dozens or hundreds of contempt cases, we are dealing with a major problem?

Let the opponents of the bill lay their cards on the table. Are they implying that mass disregard to court orders lies ahead in the administration of this bill?

Let us assume for a moment there will be mass contempt of court. How are we to respond? Are we to say, by adopting this amendment, that juries chosen on an unrepresentative basis are to be interposed between the courts and their orders on one hand and defendants bound by those orders on the other? If

[10] For further comment on Morse as speaker, see *Representative American Speeches: 1946-47*, p 153-8, "The Independent in Politics"; *1956-57*, p93-108, "Constitutional Liberalism and the Democratic Party."

we are dealing with threatened mass contempt, do we not owe it to the orderly administration of justice to maintain its traditional defense—the contempt power?

On the other hand, if contempts are expected to be few and isolated, what is the clamor to impose limitations on contempt cases to which the United States is a party that do not now exist under the law and have not heretofore been imposed?

We are told that trial by jury is an inviolable right. But the courts have held otherwise and the statutes are to the contrary, as I pointed out in my speech on Tuesday.

There is no constitutional right to trial by jury in contempt cases. There is no due process requirement of trial by jury in contempt cases. The contempt power is the power of courts to require compliance with decrees and to punish for willful refusal to comply. Why? The right exists so that the courts will not be flouted and that individuals will not take the law into their own hands.

It has been contended that the law since 1914 requires jury trial in all cases of criminal contempt. That is not so. The Clayton Act provisions requiring jury trial for criminal contempts apply only to those cases in which the violation of the court decree is also a violation of a criminal statute of the United States or a state. The elements of a criminal contempt are willful disobedience and punishment which cannot be avoided by later compliance. The factor, under the Clayton Act, which has been applied to all classes of criminal contempt, and not merely violations of antitrust law decrees, requiring jury trial, is that the violation of the decree is also an act which violates a criminal statute. The mere fact that the underlying case may be similar to a criminal case does not make it a certainty that criminal contempts invoke the violation of the similar criminal statute.

For example, a remedial decree may require a vote registrar to report back to the court at fixed intervals what he is doing to comply. If he willfully fails to report as directed, he would violate the decree—but not the statute prohibiting officials to discriminate in the registering of voters. Or the decree may order the official to post and publish notices as to new registry procedures. A willful refusal to follow the order could be punished as criminal contempt and yet not be a violation of a criminal statute.

A lawful order to remedy discrimination can have requirements very different from the prohibitions of a criminal statute on the same subject. So it is not accurate to say that in civil proceedings in the field in which there is also a criminal statute, trial for contempt is essentially the same as trial for violation of the criminal statute.

Even beyond that, the purpose of the trials is different. Sentence for violation of the statute is punishment for the transgression of law. Punishment for willful contempt of a court order is in vindication of the court's authority to require compliance of orders presumptively valid.

In most cases, the order of a lower court is stayed until an appeal can be filed and consummated. Only pressing requirements for action cause courts to deny applications for a stay. But if a court in its sound discretion does deny a stay, is that any reason for giving special treatment to defendants who do what they please in violation of the order? Assuredly not.

There has been a good deal of sloganizing on the right to a trial by jury, but the slogans do not bear up under legal analysis.

There have been stirring defenses of the jury as a shield against despotism. As I said earlier in this debate, juries have their utility. But have they in fact and in deed proven to be a guardian always against tyranny?

Take an example from our own history. No laws ever enacted have earned the just opprobrium of our people equal to the revulsion to the Alien and Sedition Acts. The Alien Act never resulted in a prosecution, although it drove outspoken aliens out of the country.

But the Sedition Act of 1798 resulted in ten cases of prosecution, with a possible eleventh, which is not thoroughly documented.

The Sedition Act was directed against a free press and free speech under the guise of condemning seditious libel. The act was used by the Federalists in power to silence opposition newspapers and political opponents. Most of the defendants were newspaper publishers, writers, or pamphleteers who were critical of President John Adams. One defendant was a Representative from Vermont, Matthew Lyon. Another defendant was Anthony Haswell, editor of a newspaper, who published an advertisement to raise funds for Lyon's fine, and who said some strong things about Lyon's conviction and the unfair treatment he was receiving as a prisoner.

All ten defendants were tried by juries which, under the Sedition Act, had the authority to decide both the law and the facts. A reading of the contemporary accounts of the trials—see Wharton, *State Trials of the United States*—some based on shorthand reports, clearly show how the defendants were prevented from presenting their defense adequately. The kangaroo-court methods were obvious and shocking.

What did the juries do in all ten cases? They convicted the defendants. (The law expired automatically in two years and no appeals were taken.) —Anderson—*The Enforcement of the Alien and Sedition Laws, Report of the American Historical Association,* 1912. In one case the jury deliberated one hour—Wharton, page 336. In the Virginia trial of Callender the jury brought in the guilty verdict after two hours.

The Sedition Act is acknowledged to have been the most tyrannical in our history, both in substance and in application. In all the cases tried under it, the jury system failed utterly to function as the guardian of freemen's liberties. I do not recount this history to impugn the jury system. I merely cite it to show that the jury system does not have the celestial virtues claimed for it in this debate.

The jury system was abused in these cases. Federal marshals, who summoned juries, selected Federalist sympathizers for seats on the juries. The juries in these cases were not fully representative, just as jury panels are not truly representative of communities where they are based on voters' lists which are unrepresentative or are based upon discrimination because of the color of the skin.

The Sedition Act cases do not show that juries will always convict. We know that is not so. They do show that juries are not proof against passion and prejudice—political, sentimental, or otherwise. That there are juries, such as that in Clinton, which can be dispassionate, I do not doubt.

All I claim about this issue is the following:

First. Jury trial does not have the virtues claimed for it;

Second. There is not a constitutional requirement for jury trial in contempt cases;

Third. There is not a due process requirement of trial by jury;

Fourth. Criminal contempt does not necessarily involve violation of criminal statutes;

Fifth. If there is to be massive resistance to court decrees in civil rights cases, we should not hobble the courts as they have never been hobbled before;

Sixth. If, as is usual, criminal contempt cases under this law will be rare, the dispute over trial by jury has been disproportionate to the issue and has unfortunately obscured the underlying purpose of the proposed legislation—namely, additional and effective civil proceedings to protect the rights of millions of citizens.

I believe, and I speak most respectfully, that the advocates of jury trial in this debate have misplaced their zeal. Some have permitted themselves to be distracted by an issue with apparent appeal, but little substance. Let us return to our task—the insurance of basic rights to a people who have yet to be permitted to get past the waiting room of citizenship.

Let us remember throughout the rest of the debate on this issue that, after all, it is for the courts to determine the issue as to whether a constitutional civil right is being denied any American, irrespective of the color of his or her skin.

EDUCATION

FEDERAL COURT ORDERS MUST BE UPHELD [1]

DWIGHT D. EISENHOWER [2]

President Dwight D. Eisenhower gave this address to the nation over the national radio and television networks, on Tuesday evening, September 24, 1957.

The President was attempting to justify his order calling out Federal troops to defend the integration program at Little Rock, Arkansas, Central High School. Here was the first instance since Reconstruction days of resort to Federal force to compel equality of treatment for the Negroes of the South.

The President's action was the culmination of the previous two weeks of legal and political efforts of Governor Orval Faubus of Arkansas and his colleagues to thwart integration in the Little Rock schools.

The local school board had planned for school integration to begin in 1957, to be completed in 1963. A petition from citizens to the State Chancery Court to halt the integration was overruled by Judge Ronald N. Davies, of the Federal District Court. On September 3, under Governor Faubus' orders, the National Guard surrounded Central High, "to maintain order," and to bar the nine Negro students from entering the school. Judge Davies later issued a Federal injunction for the Governor to appear on September 20 to explain his interference with Federal court orders.

The Governor consulted President Eisenhower on September 14, at Newport, Rhode Island. On September 20, Faubus withdrew the troops. On the following Monday mobs milled about the school, and became even more threatening on the following day, despite the President's proclamation calling upon them to desist. This was the background and the immediate occasion of the President's order for one thousand members of the 101st Airborne Division to move into Little Rock, and his speech to explain his order.

The President's persuasive techniques included his forthright explanation of the immediate order; his review of the Little Rock integration program since 1955; the Federal court orders to support this integration (logically his was a case of "This—or nothing") and the mob defiance

---

[1] Text furnished by the White House.
[2] For biographical note, see Appendix.

of the court orders. The issue which the speech pointed up then was, should anarchy and mob rule displace the order of a Federal court? The speaker further persuaded by avowing his personal kinship with and sympathy for the South, his confidence that public opinion would support his move, and his hope that foreign propaganda that decried our "democracy" would thus be thwarted.

Eisenhower's delivery had little emotional stress. It was one of his more impressive speeches.

Although the Federal troops ended the open opposition and saw to it that the nine Negro students attended classes, much of the South strongly resented the President's action. Governor Faubus, in a broadcast on September 26, referred to the "naked bayonets" and to the "miiltary occupation." Southern extremists, for example, Governor Marvin Griffin of Georgia, bitterly denounced the move as duplicating the post-Civil War occupation of the South. Many Northerners, too, criticized Eisenhower for not having made plain much earlier that he would counter by force, if necessary, deliberate flouting of Court orders. In such case, it was argued, no Little Rock defiance would have developed.

The Soviets had a wonderful propaganda holiday among all nations with their pictures of the Arkansas spectacle of racial discrimination. Undoubtedly America's basic position as the champion of human rights and equality was weakened in our foreign relations.

Later the Federal troops were withdrawn and the federalized National Guard was left to preserve order. In 1958 the issue of how and when to integrate in critical Southern communities remained.

Good evening, my fellow citizens:

For a few minutes this evening I want to speak to you about the serious situation that has arisen in Little Rock. To make this talk I have come to the President's office in the White House. I could have spoken from Rhode Island, where I have been staying recently, but I felt that, in speaking from the house of Lincoln, of Jackson and of Wilson, my words would better convey both the sadness I feel in the action I was compelled today to take and the firmness with which I intend to pursue this course until the orders of the Federal court at Little Rock can be executed without unlawful interference.

In that city, under the leadership of demagogic extremists, disorderly mobs have deliberately prevented the carrying out of proper orders from a Federal court. Local authorities have not eliminated that violent opposition and, under the law, I yesterday issued a Proclamation calling upon the mob to disperse.

This morning the mob again gathered in front of the Central High School of Little Rock, obviously for the purpose of again preventing the carrying out of the Court's order relating to the admission of Negro children to that school.

Whenever normal agencies prove inadequate to the task and it becomes necessary for the Executive Branch of the Federal Government to use its powers and authority to uphold Federal Courts, the President's responsibility is inescapable.

In accordance with that responsibility, I have today issued an Executive Order directing the use of troops under Federal authority to aid in the execution of Federal law at Little Rock, Arkansas. This became necessary when my Proclamation of yesterday was not observed, and the obstruction of justice still continues.

It is important that the reasons for my action be understood by all our citizens.

As you know, the Supreme Court of the United States has decided that separate public educational facilities for the races are inherently unequal and therefore compulsory school segregation laws are unconstitutional.

Our personal opinions about the decision have no bearing on the matter of enforcement; the responsibility and authority of the Supreme Court to interpret the Constitution are very clear. Local Federal courts were instructed by the Supreme Court to issue such orders and decrees as might be necessary to achieve admission to public schools without regard to race—and with all deliberate speed.

During the past several years, many communities in our Southern states have instituted public school plans for gradual progress in the enrollment and attendance of school children of all races in order to bring themselves into compliance with the law of the land.

They thus demonstrated to the world that we are a nation in which laws, not men, are supreme.

I regret to say that this truth—the cornerstone of our liberties—was not observed in this instance.

It was my hope that this localized situation would be brought under control by city and state authorities. If the use of local police powers had been sufficient, our traditional method of leaving the problem in those hands would have been pursued. But when large gatherings of obstructionists made it impossible for the decree of the Court to be carried out, both the law and the national interest demanded that the President take action.

Here is the sequence of events in the development of the Little Rock school case.

In May of 1955, the Little Rock School Board approved a moderate plan for the gradual desegregation of the public schools in that city. It provided that a start toward integration would be made at the present term in the high school, and that the plan would be in full operation by 1963. Here I might say that in a number of communities in Arkansas integration in the schools has already started and without violence of any kind. Now this Little Rock plan was challenged in the courts by some who believed that the period of time as proposed in the plan was too long.

The United States Court at Little Rock, which has supervisory responsibility under the law for the plan of desegregation in the public schools, dismissed the challenge, thus approving a gradual rather than an abrupt change from the existing system. The court found that the school board had acted in good faith in planning for a public school system free from racial discrimination.

Since that time, the court has on three separate occasions issued orders directing that the plan be carried out. All persons were instructed to refrain from interfering with the efforts of the school board to comply with the law.

Proper and sensible observance of the law then demanded the respectful obedience which the nation has a right to expect from all its people. This, unfortunately, has not been the case at Little Rock. Certain misguided persons, many of them imported into Little Rock by agitators, have insisted upon defying the law and have sought to bring it into disrepute. The orders of the court have thus been frustrated.

The very basis of our individual rights and freedoms rests upon the certainty that the President and the Executive Branch of Government will support and insure the carrying out of the decisions of the Federal Courts, even, when necessary, with all the means at the President's command.

Unless the President did so, anarchy would result.

There would be no security for any except that which each one of us could provide for himself.

The interest of the nation in the proper fulfillment of the law's requirements cannot yield to opposition and demonstrations by some few persons.

Mob rule cannot be allowed to override the decisions of our courts.

Now, let me make it very clear that Federal troops are not being used to relieve local and state authorities of their primary duty to preserve the peace and order of the community. Nor are the troops there for the purpose of taking over the responsibility of the School Board and the other responsible local officials in running Central High School. The running of our school system and the maintenance of peace and order in each of our states are strictly local affairs and the Federal Government does not interfere except in a very few special cases and when requested by one of the several states. In the present case the troops are there, pursuant to law, solely for the purpose of preventing interference with the orders of the court.

The proper use of the powers of the Executive Branch to enforce the orders of a Federal court is limited to extraordinary and compelling circumstances. Manifestly, such an extreme situation has been created in Little Rock. This challenge must be met and with such measures as will preserve to the people as a whole their lawfully-protected rights in a climate permitting their free and fair exercise.

The overwhelming majority of our people in every section of the country are united in their respect for observance of the law—even in those cases where they may disagree with that law.

They deplore the call of extremists to violence.

The decision of the Supreme Court concerning school integration, of course, affects the South more seriously than it does other sections of the country. In that region I have many warm friends, some of them in the city of Little Rock. I have deemed it a great personal privilege to spend in our Southland tours of duty while in the military service and enjoyable recreational periods since that time.

So from intimate personal knowledge, I know that the overwhelming majority of the people in the South—including those of Arkansas and of Little Rock—are of good will, united in their efforts to preserve and respect the law even when they disagree with it.

They do not sympathize with mob rule. They, like the rest of our nation, have proved in two great wars their readiness to sacrifice for America.

A foundation of our American way of life is our national respect for law.

In the South, as elsewhere, citizens are keenly aware of the tremendous disservice that has been done to the people of Arkansas in the eyes of the nation, and that has been done to the nation in the eyes of the world.

At a time when we face grave situations abroad because of the hatred that communism bears toward a system of government based on human rights, it would be difficult to exaggerate the harm that is being done to the prestige and influence, and indeed to the safety, of our nation and the world.

Our enemies are gloating over this incident and using it everywhere to misrepresent our whole nation. We are portrayed as a violator of those standards of conduct which the peoples of the world united to proclaim in the Charter of the United Nations. There they affirmed "faith in fundamental human rights" and "in the dignity and worth of the human person" and they did so "without distinction as to race, sex, language or religion."

And so, with deep confidence, I call upon the citizens of the state of Arkansas to assist in bringing to an immediate end all interference with the law and its processes. If resistance to the Federal court orders ceases at once, the further presence of Federal troops will be unnecessary and the city of Little Rock will return to its normal habits of peace and order and a blot upon the fair name and high honor of our nation will be removed.

Thus will be restored the image of America and of all its parts as one nation, indivisible, with liberty and justice for all.

Good night, and thank you very much.

MEMO TO THE CLASS OF 1957:
OUR ECONOMIC WORLD AND YOU [3]

G. Keith Funston [4]

President G. Keith Funston, of the New York Stock Exchange, gave this address at the Commencement exercises at the University of Maryland, at College Park, Maryland, on Saturday morning, June 8, 1957.

The speaker, as is obvious from his remarks, is a former educator, was president of Trinity College, Hartford, Connecticut, and for some years before that appointment was a member of the teaching staff at Trinity. Also, from his general thesis of the graduate and his economic role, and from the details of this speech, it was obvious that the speaker was an experienced business executive as well as a graduate of the Harvard Business School. Funston's concrete specifications suggested by employers for those wishing to qualify on executive teams were based upon his own experience with the American Radiator and Standard Sanitary Corporation, Sylvania Electric Products, Inc., and similar firms.

The entire address has oral quality—as if it had been uttered extemporaneously and later recorded as given. The speaker at no point loses direct communication with the graduates before him. The speech is well organized, with the chief points headlined for readers and orally stressed for full understanding by the listener-observers.

The speaker, however, really gives three speeches. The first one deals with economic education in general. "You will be expected to demonstrate an articulate awareness of how our economic system works, why it has taken us as far as it has, and what can be done to improve it." Those who analyze the economic education of undergraduates, the structure of our economic system, the explanation of its trends, and the principles and policies to improve it would want the speaker to give an entire speech to such diagnosis and solution.

The speaker's second speech lies in his treatment of "women's economic problems." [5]

The third speech, and Funston's main point, is contained in the section on what employers expect of college graduates of today who are to take over as members of the executive teams.

[3] Text furnished through the cooperation of Paul Kalton, Director of Public Relations of the New York Stock Exchange. Reprinted here through the courtesy of President G. Keith Funston.

[4] For biographical note, see Appendix.

[5] Compare this with Funston's talk on General Credit Controls before the Women's Press Club, Washington D.C., October 2, 1957, reprinted in *Vital Speeches of the Day*, 24:89-92, November 15, 1957.

Funston's well rounded educational philosophy is expressed in his final point in which he links economic skills and understanding with the broad responsibilities of political and moral association.

The speech moves briskly, reveals its author's interesting personality, and becomes also good material for the reading public.

These graduates of June 1957 by the year's end found themselves amidst vast economic and political disturbances created by the Sputniks, the further economic and political clashes in the Middle and Far East, the spasmodic declines of the stock market itself, the shrinkages of billions in market values, and the economic uncertainties of 1958.

A few months ago President Elkins told you that the university's problem is to develop a quantity of quality. As I sense the expectations that envelop you today, I can't help but feel that your president's problem is well on the way towards being solved.

I am deeply honored to be here and to play a small part in the great tradition of this University. I have especially looked forward to joining you. First, to offer you my sincere congratulations and, second, to take part in celebrating this centennial and sesquicentennial anniversary.

At commencement time particularly, I am proud of my own deep feelings about the educational process and what it means to us. Almost one hundred years ago James Russell Lowell expressed it beautifully. He said: "It was in making education not only common to all, but in some sense compulsory *on* all, that the destiny of the free republic was practically settled."

Despite my wholehearted agreement, I must also admit to some rather mixed emotions. They stem, I suspect, from the bittersweet quality that always accompanies my return to a college campus. On the one hand, it's always a thrill to come back, if only briefly. On the other, my own years at Trinity—even my undergraduate years—don't usually seem so far behind. But this weekend is my class's twenty-fifth anniversary. And each passing commencement makes me appreciate how long ago 1932 really was.

In this connection, I have begun to feel something like the veteran movie producer whose name is a household word in America. At the age of seventy-one he summoned his top executives to discuss plans for the future. A dedication of effort, he told them, a unanimity in executing their bold programs would be needed. "I ask this not for myself," he sighed. "After all, I'm seventy-one now. And at seventy-one, how many more years are left to me—maybe twenty-two or twenty-three!"

Well, the productive years left to you are only beginning. More than that, I am absolutely convinced those years will treat you well. For one thing, your training here has equipped you, more admirably than you realize, for the immediate steps ahead. Moreover, society today puts its greatest premium on precisely those skills and qualities your faculty has struggled to develop— the ability to think, to question and to perceive.

College Graduates Are Nation's Best-Advertised Shortage: They Face New Responsibilities, Much Greater Opportunities in Expanding U.S. Economy

All this, I admit, may seem very small comfort right now. Most of you are on the verge of leaving the academic cloisters. Whether the next step is military service, a job or marriage it is the most difficult and responsible move you have yet undertaken.

The pressures and tensions you feel about this are very real indeed. They are also understandable—and they must be recognized and coped with. There is, perhaps, some consolation in knowing that for graduates everywhere the wave of excitement always seems to alternate with the wave of anxiety. It is part of the price we pay for moving ahead.

Nothing has so dramatized this fact for me as a recent experience at the New York Stock Exchange. We had invited a well-known American artist to bring a representative group of his students from Pratt Institute to sketch and capture the excitement of our trading floor. To our surprise, his group consisted solely of third-year students. Freshmen and sophomores, he explained, showed fine promise, but their talents were not yet developed. Juniors, on the other hand, had come into their own. Their drawings were free, clear and expressive. And the seniors? Well, they hadn't been brought along, he said, because their recent work reflected the fact that they were only weeks away from graduation. Their efforts had become labored and inhibited. His seniors obviously reflected their pressing concern about the immediacy of their next move—making a living.

In like terms, I can recognize the things that probably concern you most today. And in preparing these remarks, I have tried to put myself in your shoes. I have posed the same questions that perhaps are troubling you. Questions like: What's ahead? What are my chances? What will it be like, earning a living or running a home? And perhaps the most important question of all—since it sums up everything else: What's expected of me in our economic world.

Well, I would do you a disservice if I said the answers were simple. But I should like to try to put them in perspective.

For one thing, even the most casual newspaper reader knows that in the arena into which you are moving, peace has a delicate toehold. There is the threat of the bomb. There is great poverty in some areas. But there are important counter-balances. Statesmen the world over are struggling, in good faith, to avert war. Medical miracles promise longer, healthier lives. In many lands, notably in America, living standards are higher than ever. Our factories are turning out more goods. Our people have more money to spend and to save. Finally, enormous changes—most of them to the good—are continuing to shape our future. And these changes have an immediate bearing on you.

In the years it has taken you to go from kindergarten through college, multibillion dollar industries have grown up with you: electronics, synthetics, rocket fuels and rocket engines are just a few of your contemporaries.

And in this process of growth, you—as college graduates—have become the nation's best-advertised shortage. There is an urgent need for college-trained people to handle our advanced technology. And I don't by any means mean just technically-trained people. For our real need is for the full man—for those who are adaptable, imaginative and trained to think.

A great industrialist, Benjamin Fairless, summed this up not long ago. He commented wryly that with our new automation, detail work may well disappear into the innards of a computer.

But he added: "If the apple which fell on Sir Isaac Newton's head had happened to fall on a Univac, the machine might have blown a tube . . . but it never would have come up with the law of gravity." No, machines will not do our thinking. For that job, we need people who are essentially creative. And the place we are most likely to find them is on the campuses of our colleges.

One final fact that is likely to influence your immediate future is the quiet, economic revolution that has taken place in the United States. Perhaps it has passed your notice. But at the Stock Exchange we have been in the midst of it, exerting all of our efforts to encourage it soundly.

Simply stated, it is the growth of a new kind of capitalism— a People's Capitalism. In it, men and women from every walk of life have begun to invest directly in the ownership of our great businesses. Today, more than 8.5 million people—two thirds of them with incomes under $7,500 a year—are the owners of our publicly-held companies. This is a 33 per cent jump over 1952. (And if the owners of private corporations are added, the stockholder family would swell to over 10 million.) In addition, some 110 million people are indirect owners of our corporations through their investments in life insurance companies, savings banks and pension funds.

The significance of this last economic development is twofold and worth exploring for a moment. *First,* by encouraging greater shareownership—by giving people everywhere the chance to participate more directly in the risks and rewards of our economy—we are proving the preposterousness of the Marxist theory. That theory, you'll recall, held that the rich will get richer while the poor become poorer. Well, we are actually demonstrating in America, as one economist has noted, that "of all the great industrial nations, the one that clings most tenaciously to private capitalism has come closest to the Socialist goal of providing abundance for all in a classless society."

I would like to make one aside here. It is worth noting that recently the Kremlin announced that Russian workers would no longer have to subscribe to the government's savings bond program. This was an unexpected windfall for young people like yourselves who had been forced to commit as much as two months' pay each year to bond purchases. But coupled with this order was the statement that Russia would no longer pay interest on savings bonds outstanding. For older people this stunning announcement meant wiping out a source of income they had counted on to sustain them in later years. It is little wonder that in defending his action, Mr. Khruschev anticipated that capitalist countries wouldn't understand this new action. I believe we understand it much better than he would like us to.

And this brings up the second reason why our own move to broaden shareownership is important. It is increasingly clear that the economic freedom running through our lives has a strong relationship to the other freedoms we enjoy. To a large degree, the strength of our economy is the key to a more secure world. And for our kind of capitalism to remain strong we need the understanding and active support of thoughtful, trained people like yourselves.

Thus, I return to the major question I have posed: What's expected of you in our economic world? In a large measure the answer is you will be expected to demonstrate an articulate awareness of how our economic system works, why it has taken us as far as it has, and what can be done to improve it still further.

Women Play Dominant Role as Managers of the Nation's Purse Strings: Today's Coeds Will Be Called on to Deal with Wide Range of Complex Economic Problems

Let me be specific.

The responsibility for being economically aware is by no means confined to those of the class of 1957 who will be occupying the breadwinner's role. *All* of you will be drawing your livelihood from American enterprise. And all of you—sooner than you possibly expect—will be acquiring a certain ownership in that enterprise.

For the coeds among you whose next job involves running a home, this will mean dealing with problems a great deal more complex than managing a weekly food budget or balancing a check book—though both of these unusual talents will be enormously appreciated by your husbands.

It will mean responding also to the demands that your husband's work will almost certainly place on you personally. You will be expected, for example, to provide a sympathetic and understanding car to forgive the havoc that working late and traveling will create in your own cherished social plans.

Women, too, are willy-nilly becoming the possessors of our financial earth. This last statement needs no more amplification than the fact that women own about half of our savings accounts and government bonds. They constitute a substantial portion of people owning life insurance. And finally, women actually outnumber men as shareowners in the nation's businesses—by some 52-to-48 per cent. The financial importance women enjoy—along with the profound satisfaction of raising our families—gives added meaning to the old observation: that when you educate a man, you educate an *individual;* when you educate a woman you educate the *whole family.*

Employers Look Ahead: Expect College Graduates of Today to Take Over as Members of Executive Teams Tomorrow

The majority of this class of 1957 will, of course, be changing cap and gown for roles in business and industry. I have mentioned briefly the way businessmen feel about you. I suspect there is no mistaking the earnestness with which many of you already have been wooed and won by this company or that.

It is fair to add a word about the enthusiasm of your prospective employers. They are looking beyond the immediate present. They have the certain knowledge that the future will require managerial talent in such quantities that many experts are fearful we may not be able to develop it in time. As a result, your employers are both anxious and hopeful that *you* will fill the bill. Thus, I would like to describe briefly four yardsticks they will use to measure your progress. These, indeed, are a guide as to what is expected of you.

One: Your employer will look for *people who can get along with others.* He wants men and women who can respond to new situations while still maintaining their individual points of view. He will expect, moreover, that you will operate within the framework of an organization. Much has been written about that badly-abused term—"teamwork." Well, years ago Andrew Carnegie put it in proper perspective when he said bluntly: "take away our factories, take away our trade, our avenues of transportation, our money. Leave us nothing but our organization and in four years we shall have reestablished ourselves. . . ."

Two: Your employer will look for *creative ability*—for the initiative and imagination required to range beyond the immediate job. And he will turn instinctively to people venturesome enough to suggest new methods of doing business because the old ways just aren't good enough. Above all, he will look for people who can tell him not only *how* something should be done, but also *whether* or not it should be done at all.

Three: Your employer will look, at the same time, for *people with measured judgment*. He will seek those with the patience to learn their business thoroughly, the calm ability to get all the facts, and the skill to relate them to the broader economic and social problems that press in on a company. I would emphasize, in this connection, that obviously no company today operates in a vacuum. It is part of the community in which it lives. It is responsible to shareowners, employees, customers and suppliers. Thus, a company's decisions are frequently made against a background of facts that are far removed from strictly dollar considerations. And to help make these decisions a company needs broad-gauge people.

Finally: Your employer will look for men and women with *firm beliefs and the ability to articulate them*. He will expect people with courage—willing to cling to basic convictions and equally willing to express new ones. He will expect a mature understanding of our free economy and its relationships to the other freedoms we enjoy.

Of these, I would stress the third point—the necessity for getting the facts—because it is so well illustrated by my own experience at the Stock Exchange. One of the constant battles we are waging in the financial community is against tipsters, rumor-mongers and get-rich-quick promoters. There is no future in buying gold bricks and no easy road to riches. We have been successful, I think, in protecting large segments of the public against many of the outrages of con men and gyp artists. This has been accomplished by warning investors and would-be investors, time and again, to get full information and seek sound advice before risking their investment dollars. But despite our progress, one of our sad conclusions is that we cannot protect a man either from his own cupidity or from his *failure* to exercise the most elementary form of good judgment. And these are failures which, in a broader career sense, you must avoid at all costs.

Vigilance in Protection of Basic Freedoms: Active Participation in Community—Primary Responsibilities in a Changing, Challenging World

In essence, the question of judgment is one you will have to weigh day-after-day, in many forms, and regardless of the nature of your role.

It is *your* particular role, of course, that interests *you* most today. And I would summarize your opportunities and responsibilities this way:

You are moving into a world filled with enormous change and great promise. In economic terms you can anticipate the excitement of helping shape a system of enterprise that is now in the midst of a unique revolution—characterized by a rise of a true People's Capitalism. You have the wonderful reassurance of knowing that your talents, energies and understanding are in great demand. But by the same token, very special burdens will be placed on you.

At work you will be charged with decisions requiring not only good judgment, but courage as well in exercising it. Behind these decisions there will have to be an *awareness* that our economic freedoms are part and parcel of our other freedoms. And you will be called on to demonstrate an *understanding* of the changes—such as broader shareownership—that now are shaping society.

At home, your burden will be no less arduous. You will be introduced to the job of managing a household, raising children, planning savings programs and investing wisely—not only in securities—but in your futures as well.

There is no question in my mind that your years at Maryland have prepared you well for this. In the long view of history your record will, I think, give fresh meaning to Lowell's observation that ". . . in making education not only common to all, but in some sense compulsory on all . . . the destiny of the free republic of America was practically settled."

Congratulations and Godspeed.

TALK TO UNDERGRADUATES [6]

J. ROBERT OPPENHEIMER [7]

Dr. J. Robert Oppenheimer, director of the Institute for Advanced Study in Princeton, New Jersey, gave this talk at the California Institute of Technology, Pasadena, March 4, 1957. He was the first 1957 visitor in the California Tech YMCA's "Leaders of America" program. From February 28 to March 5 he spent most of his time in informal discussions with students. "Talk to Undergraduates" was his one formal address during his visit.

The speaker, the son of a German-Jewish immigrant, completed the four-year A.B. program at Harvard in three years. He was graduated with Phi Beta Kappa and *summa cum laude* honors. His postgraduate studies in theoretical physics were at the University of Cambridge, Göttingen (where he received the Ph.D. degree), Harvard, California Institute of Technology, Leyden, and Zurich. Later he taught at the University of California and at California Tech.

His national and international fame came in 1943-1945, when he was in charge of the Los Alamos A-Bomb project.

He stated (in a letter of March 4, 1954) that prior to about 1940 he had read little in economics or politics and had no radio or telephone. But he studied Sanskrit, and read widely in classics, novels, plays, poetry, as well as in his special field of nuclear physics.

In 1947 he was appointed director and professor of physics at the Institute for Advanced Study at Princeton. In that year he was appointed chairman of the Advisory Committee to the Atomic Energy Commission. In late 1953 President Eisenhower directed that a "blank wall be placed between Dr. Oppenheimer and secret data," pending a security review. The charges were that he had associated with Communists, had hired them at Los Alamos, had contributed money to Communist organizations, and had opposed the H-Bomb project. He was not accused of betraying his trust by giving secret information to the Communists or of being a Communist party member. The Atomic Energy Commission, Rear Admiral Lewis Strauss, chairman, on June 29, 1954, by a vote of four to one, sustained the charges against Oppenheimer, and he was denied free access to restricted information and held as a "bad security risk." Commissioner Henry D. Smyth against his four colleagues called for Oppenheimer's reinstatement and declared that his "loyalty and trustworthiness emerge clearly" from his full record in governmental services.

[6] Text from *Engineering and Science Monthly*. March 1957. Published at the California Institute of Technology. Reprinted here through the courtesy of Dr. J. Robert Oppenheimer and with permission of the *Engineering and Science Monthly*.

[7] For biographical note, see Appendix.

After 1953 Oppenheimer continued at his Princeton post. The Institute's twenty-six members issued a statement of confidence in "his loyalty and patriotic devotion."

Oppenheimer as a speaker was nervously alert. Here and there in his remarks in the address below he was introspective; always he was reflective and creative.

I have spent enough time here so that not all of you are complete strangers to me; but this is the first opportunity I have had to say some things which, though formal, are nonetheless very much heartfelt. I thank you for asking me out; I think it an honor. Those of you who have met with me, and seen me struggling with questions to which I did not know the answers, must be aware of the fact that I have had many misgivings as to whether I rated the honor. I want to thank you for the very great friendliness, the very great frankness and the earnestness with which you have dealt with me. And I would like to thank you for adding a little to my understanding of the world we live in.

I have a few thoughts on the situation we face that I would like to talk about tonight. Of course, what I say is not only incomplete and partial, but there is a very special ground for some humility in what I do say. Between your generation and mine there are differences that neither of us is likely fully to understand. I am aware of this gulf and I don't underestimate it.

There is another reason for humility: What you have to deal with is partly the heritage of what the generations your senior have left you. I think we have no great reason for pride in the heritage. The problems seem to me very grave, and the measures and means for dealing with them and resolving them nothing to write home about.

Before talking about the specific problems of learning and ignorance—as they appear here, and as they appear in a larger sense for all of us—it may not be too bad to remind ourselves of some of the peculiarities of the time. It seems to me an extremely peculiar age. All ages are; but I am in some doubt as to whether there is any valid historical analog to this time.

I was reminded today of a story; and before outlining some of the traits of the mid-twentieth century, I may repeat it. It has a kind of moral, I think. A friend of mine signed up in the Army, after Pearl Harbor. He is a Greek philologist and philosopher, and the Army understood that he was a clever man and put him to work in Intelligence. Part of his job, in preparation for the invasion of Europe, was to interview men who had participated in the Canadian raid and in the evacuation from Dunkirk, and one day he talked to a fellow who had been the communications officer for his outfit This fellow had come moderately late to Dunkirk and there were great masses of men on the beach waiting to be evacuated. So he dug down in the sand and turned on his radio and listened. There was a little bit of music—and that was all right—and then he got a BBC broadcast. The broadcast described how the ships were standing off to sea, waiting, and the men were waiting in long lines, and the Germans were approaching, and overhead there were dogfights—and the fellow said, "It was much too horrible; I had to turn it off."

So it is whenever we take an appraisal of our situation. One of the features of this time is that we live under a palpable threat of an apocalypse. I have talked with you enough so that you know that I don't regard this as inevitable; on the contrary, I think that for anyone who has an opportunity of working to avert it, that is a valid full-time job. It isn't like the apocalypse that was expected in the year 1000, but it is very much at the back of our minds in everything we do.

It is a strange time, too, in that never in the history of the world has there been as rapid a growth of knowledge, as rapid a growth in understanding, or as great changes. I suppose that, in the eighteenth century, men talked about how knowledge doubled every fifty years. I think we could make a case for saying that it doubled every ten years now.

This creates problems of which I will talk mostly tonight. But it also creates problems of the use of that knowledge, of the vast powers that it seems to make available, of the choices. It creates a world of incredibly rapid change. Almost nobody can look back to a schooling with a feeling that it is entirely relevant to the problems that he is now dealing with. Almost everyone has to have the sense that he goes to school all his life.

In some ways, this situation, which I think is a natural continuation of the fluidity and openness of American society—an openness now not with regard to the physical frontier, but with regard to the frontier of knowledge—has given this country a strange destiny. I cannot believe that other parts of the world will not also very rapidly be caught up in changes comparable to those in which we live. They are not prepared for it; they have remained in relatively steady, relatively quiet, relatively enduring forms. And how we deal with this, certainly will not be an example that other peoples will inevitably or rightly follow. But how we deal with it cannot be irrelevant to the future of the whole world.

This is also a time when the very rapidity of change seems to me to underline the irony that is so characteristic of history— the irony which makes the event, the outcome, so different from the human purpose.

Think of the Communist movement; it began in compassion, and now it is probably the least compassionate of any major political force the world has seen for a long, long time. Think of China, with its pattern of respect and love for the family and the past, its addiction to reflection, and almost private beauty. Think what the Chinese have embraced in the way of forced, quick, violent, brilliant change—and how little they are prepared for it. Think of India, if you will, and a government in India which is a direct consequence of Cambridge, of Oxford and of London—these symbols of two centuries of oppression. And think of us, who founded ourselves in independence, and who are inextricably stuck in the most monstrous kind of interdependence—both here, where the vastness of all our affairs makes the individual's wink invisible, and even interdependent with very remote parts of the globe. Think of the irony of the great weapons, which, developed to give a military answer to the problem of security, have assumed such proportions that they almost cannot be used, and have produced for the general staffs that evoked them a nightmare of almost total insecurity.

All these things—and there are many more—could easily, it seems to me, make in the times a kind of bitterness and a kind of feeling that the individual had better see to his own delight and to heck with society, to heck with virtue. That is not so different from the way it was in the decade when I grew up, after the First World War, where a kind of revolt was characteristic in the colleges, and in the arts. It was a revolt which said that what we have had from the past was not much of a guide for the future, a revolt where there was a hope of improvising something gay and new, where the bitter fruit of that terrible war seemed to call for a kind of new, fresh departure.

It isn't really quite like that now. I think that today, if I know you and your friends through the country, you hold very close to the ancient imperatives—the imperatives of Christianity, of our traditions, of our country. I think you are not after novelty and improvisation in art or politics or philosophy, or manners. I think that, even if the end of our time should come, you are quite content that we live out these days faithful to the gospels, faithful to the ethic, faithful to the sense of responsibility, which we have from times past.

These are some of the things that are in the background. Of course, the present problem of young people at college is the same everywhere. They are finding their way into an enormous cognitive jungle, the jungle of everything there is to know. They are finding their way into it with very little guide, either from synoptic kinds of knowledge, like philosophy, which say: This is important; this is unimportant; this fits in here; this fits in there—or from the state of the world, which doesn't, in any very clear or loud voice, say: Learn this; ignore that; learn this well; skip over that lightly.

There is, in most places, the vast trouble of impossible choices. I have talked with and been among undergraduates—and school boys and graduate students as well—in some places around the country, and a typical agony is: "What do I do? Where am I headed?" The complement of that, of course, is to be told what to do, and in a measure, that is what goes on here. I think it varies from place to place, and there is no doubt that Cal Tech is far on one side of the spectrum—of the spectrum between openness and permissiveness on the one hand, and rather strict and specific guidance on the other; between knowledge as an end in itself, something to study because of the joy of it and the beauty of it—and knowledge as an instrument, as a way of getting on in the future. I think Cal Tech is very much on the instrumental side, and very much on the predetermined side.

But the sense of loss which I hear in you—I don't know whether it is exaggerated in our talk but I'm sure it's there—of the things which you are not studying; the sense of loss at all that you might be learning, and aren't; the slight fear that this might not be easy to make up at a later time; this is a much larger thing, a quite general part of human life. There is much more that one might know than any of us are ever going to know. There is much more to know than any of us are ever going to catch up with; and this is not just the trivial fact that we don't work hard enough; it is not the trivial fact that things are difficult to learn. It is that any form of knowledge really precludes other forms; that any serious study of one thing cuts out some other part of your life. Narrowness is not an accident of one place, but it is a condition of knowledge.

I think myself that, with the growth of knowledge—the immense perplexity, the pervasive mutual relevance of different things to each other—all we can do is to accept the state of affairs, to affirm it and to accept it deeply. It is not that some courses are not better than others and some worse, some even good and some evil; it is that, in the balance between ignorance and loss on the one hand, and knowledge and richness of experience on the other, we have to keep the affirmative love of the knowledge and the richness very close and never deny that most of what men can know, we don't know; that much of what man can know, nobody knows.

Of course, in a certain sense, this is trivial and people have always known it. When it comes to the will, the element of choice has always been clear. The fact that you had one course which precluded another; you could take a job, or you could continue to study; you could marry, or you could say goodbye; everybody knows that. But I think it has not been quite as clear how, in the very conditions of knowledge, choice is built in and exclusion is part of depth.

I don't want to try to derive this from anything in science because it seems to me quite deep and quite commonsensical, and very much a part of all our experience. But I do want to give three examples from three different areas in science which illustrate it rather sharply. One is from the physiology of perception, one is from the psychology of learning, and one is from physics.

The philosophers like to talk about sense data as though they were something that came to all men who were properly constituted, a replica, a picture, a sign of something outside; and all philosophers have always been very confident that the sense datum was something very solid to build on. But, in being able to perceive, we take a far more active part, and not necessarily a conscious one.

There is, for instance, an experiment of great simplicity having to do with hearing. The nerves running from the hair cells in a dog's ear toward the cortex can be tapped, and one can see what kind of electrical impulses travel along them. And if you take a dog so "hooked up," you will soon learn to recognize the electrical pattern of the signal that comes along when the dog hears a bell ring. If you put a piece of meat in front of the dog, that signal disappears. The way this happens is that, along with the afferent nerve fibers, there are finer nerve fibers which, so to speak, tell the nerves what to do, what to hear and what signals to send. This is not understood in detail. But the coding which we always assume characterizes the human brain—the organization of material, the focusing of attention, animadversion, concentration, memory—this coding pervades the most primitive parts of the cognitive system, and the dog may or may not hear the bell. It isn't something that he fixes up inside himself; it is a question of what he is attuned to.

There are very similar experiments, having to do, for instance, with language—a whole series of them reported from the Harvard Cognition Project. It is astonishing what people will notice and what they will ignore. For instance, if you take some sounds that have some variations in them and say them, then an American who is attuned only to our language will hear differences—but only those differences which correspond to the way we spell and write, to our phonetic elements. Of course, we don't spell and write very accurately, but we recognize *a* as distinct from *e*, and *r* as distinct from *n* and so on. If you take a Navaho who doesn't know English, he will hear quite different things. He won't distinguish our vowels, but he will distinguish by the length of the vowel. You can teach the Navaho to notice the English differences and the American to notice the Navaho differences, but he doesn't normally do it. The possibilty of communicating, of course, rests on the fact that we don't hear too much. You are hearing my talk, but only that part of it which really has meaning in English. All the rest of it—the rumble and roar that goes with it—you don't hear. It isn't that you hear it and ignore it.

Of the incredibly many examples, one of the most striking comes to anyone who tries to translate the words for colors from one language to another, even two languages that are Indo-Germanic. The English words for color distinguish spectrally what we call color, by the hue. The Greek words have to do almost entirely with depth and brightness, and you can't find a Greek word for blue. You can find one that sometimes means blue. All these questions of animadversion are extremely primitive.

And what is the example from physics? It is the one that I talk about much too much. Of course, if one is now learning atomic theory, one learns Schroedinger's equation in quantum mechanics, and it all seems very unphilosophical and practical. It is a wonderful way of describing atomic phenomena, and one tries to get the techniques and get it over with. But to anyone who lived with the development of this, it was quite a different story, because what one had to get through his head was something quite odd.

We are used to a world in which we can find out anything of interest about a large physical system without in any way questioning the means by which we can find it out. The classical examples are that we can tell where a planet is, and, by observing it successively, we can tell how fast it is moving. The question whether this observation could have any paradoxical features in it never arises. But in atomic mechanics, we had to learn that, although experiments in some ways like finding where a planet is, and in some ways like finding out its velocity, are indeed possible, and are indeed part of describing what is going on. The kind of arrangement that is suitable for doing one of these experiments not only makes it impossible to do the other, but makes it logically contradictory to assume that the other quantity has value, or has one of a number of values. In other words, we came to realize that, in the atomic scale, one can realize, by the way one goes about it in the laboratory, that there is some free choice. This is not free in the sense of an ethical problem, but just free for the physicist to decide what he is interested in or what he wants to study. Having made that choice, one has closed out the chance of doing the other thing, so that both are valid measurements, or so that he can even imagine that he has done both and that each has had a given result. If he imagines thus, and starts to draw the consequences, he will get a prediction for the future of that atom that has no relation to what he will find in the laboratory.

These are just three examples of the pervasiveness with which, in all scientific things, one meets again the fact that knowledge, by the very techniques, powers, and facts of its acquisition, by its organizing the chaos that is the world around us, precludes other knowledge.

This makes a picture of the cognitive world which, in many ways, is not the one we have inherited. It isn't as though we were in a room just looking at it, then, if we wanted to know some more, looking some more, exhausting all the properties of it, being able to talk about it all—as though we were in a temple and could go back over and over again, studying the peculiarities of the temple until there was nothing more to know, and then making a description of this room or this temple which was total and global.

It is much more as though we had deep, not always connected parts of knowledge—knowledge of physics, knowledge of life, knowledge of man, knowledge of history. Between these things that are known to any one of us, there is always potential relevance, so that one can never say, even of the most implausibly abstract kind of mathematics: This will not be relevant to psychology or physics. But the image that comes to my mind is not that of the chamber that can be exhausted, but of an essentially infinite world, knowable in many different ways; and all these paths of knowledge are interconnectable, and some are interconnected, like a great network—a great network between people, between ideas, between systems of knowledge—a reticulated kind of structure which is human culture and human society.

This means that I am very suspicious of statements that refer to totality or completeness; that I am very suspicious of our ability to have more than partial knowledge, in the very real sense that it can be supplemented and that it doesn't close. It means that I am very suspicious also of order which is hierarchical in the sense that it says that some things are more important than others—that some things are so important that you can derive everything else from them. These were great hopes of man, and philosophical systems are their monuments. I don't think that the prospects of their being realized look very good.

Now, one could take an attitude of real horror toward this and say that one can't live with it—that this is to offer man not knowledge, but chaos. I don't think that is right. We have all had the experience of seeing the relevance of something that we hadn't known before, of learning at all times in our lives something deep and new and wonderful that had been hidden before. We have all had the experience of what companionship and intercourse and an open mind can do; and I don't think the absence of global traits to our knowledge is a cause for despair. But I'd like to read you a poem that seems to me to fit a little, not only with this general situation, but perhaps even with the local situation. It is not a new poem; it is three centuries old and the language is archaic, and I can't be sure you'll like it. It is called "The Collar," and it is by a devout Anglican named George Herbert. Some of you may know it; it goes like this:

> I struck the board, and cried, No more.
>   I will abroad.
> What? Shall I ever sigh and pine?
> My lines and life are free; free as the road,
> Loose as the wind, as large as store.
>   Shall I be still in suit?
> Have I no harvest but a thorn
> To let me blood, and not restore
> What I have lost with cordial fruit?
>   Sure there was wine,

Before my sighs did dry it: there was corn,
    Before my tears did drown it.
Is the year only lost to me?
    Have I no bays to crown it?
No flowers, no garlands gay? all blasted?
    All wasted?
Not so, my heart: but there is fruit,
    And thou hast hands.
Recover all thy sigh-blown age
On double pleasures: leave thy cold dispute
Of what is fit and not; forsake thy cage,
    Thy rope of sands,
Which petty thoughts have made, and made to thee
Good cable, to enforce and draw,
    And be thy law.
While thou didst wink and wouldst not see.
    Away; take heed:
    I will abroad.
Call in thy death's-head there: tie up thy fears.
    He that forbears
    To suit and serve his need,
        Deserves his load.
But as I rav'd and grew more fierce and wild,
    At every word,
Methought I heard one calling, *Child;*
    and I replied, *My Lord.*

Having spoken so, and tried to measure what the flowering, changing, rich, but only partially ordered world of the mind means for us, it may not be inappropriate to stress what seem to me a few of the things that will be useful in living with it. They are certainly not new things; they have always been useful.

The first is to have a kind of deep reverence, not, certainly, for the learned man or the stuffed shirt, but for learning, for knowledge and skill; and to hold tight to it, and not to be talked out of it by any superficial parody of what it is, the kind of thing we learn in school where we learn to do and create and understand, and where we learn really to act with the knowledge we get.

This is something that isn't easy to come by. It hasn't been easy for man; it isn't being easy now, and it is incredibly precious; and the world is full of it. Accounts of this—stories (whether in general education or in *Life* magazine), short cuts, and synopses—miss most of the point. It is just the technique and the wonder of one's own ability to do it that is part of the value of it. And in ourselves and in other people this is, I think, to be held on to very tight. If you have learned how to be something, how to be a competent professional, you will know a great deal about what is good in this world. You will have a bond in common with every other man who is a scholar or a scientist.

The greatest of all protections against narrowness, and the greatest relief and opening, is comradeship, and that ability to learn from others of what their world is like. Learn from books for sure; learn from people, but learn with a kind of sense that every man enriches you and enlarges you if you only have the strength, the wit, the openness, the fortitude to learn what he is all about and what he knows.

And very much we need tolerance. We are all incredibly different. I think sometimes that one of the unexpected fruits of biological research may be that we can, on occasion, be made to feel more like somebody else than we normally do, and so get some impression of the immense diversity in human experience. But, of course, as it is, we don't have that. Through art, through affection, we have some sense of a global kind of what other people are like, of what life means to them, of what makes them tick, and of what their learning and their understanding is. But an immense sense of the otherness of people, and the otherness of possible worlds and ideas is, I guess, the basis of tolerance. I don't mean, in any simple way, tolerance of evil in one's self, but rather a recognition that even two people, hearing the same words, living together, seeing the same things, have some measure of gulf between them; and a recognition that when we are dealing with remote peoples, remote traditions, we need to bring an overpowering humility to our estimate of what they are, and our measure of them.

I have the impression that if we, in this time and this age, manage properly to live with the wealth of knowledge, the wealth of change, the responsibility, and the traits of impotence, which these times dish up, we will really be quite something, and that maybe there will be places and people and times that come after who will have reason to be grateful to us.

CURRENT CRISIS AND NEED FOR EDUCATION [8]

J. WILLIAM FULBRIGHT [9]

Senator J. William Fulbright (Democrat, Arkansas) gave this major speech on education in the current crisis before the Senate on January 23, 1958. Because of the length of the speech, only a section of it has been reprinted here. The student is urged to read the entire debate, interrupted as it was with questions and comments from other senators.

Senator Fulbright's criticism centered on the alleged inadequacy of President Eisenhower's program for Federal aid to education. In contrast to the President's plan for $250 million a year for four years for a scholarship-assistance plan, the Senator proposed, in addition, an authorization of $500 million a year for general aid to elementary and secondary education, to be distributed among the states on a graduated formula based on need.

The first part of the Senator's speech (most of it here omitted for lack of space) was a political attack on Eisenhower as having offered only a "printed catalog of good intentions" with which to meet the Soviet challenge. In the area of learning, Fulbright argued, would the ultimate contest between communism and free society be decided. The Prsident's State of the Union message and his later budget recommendations omitted all proposals for Federal aid to education.

Especially after the Soviet satellite launchings did educators and political leaders demand more effective results in American scientific and other education. In early 1958 the standard questions, with more thorough analysis and concrete solutions, continued: How can the needed primary and secondary school buildings, equipment, and teachers be supplied? How can the school curricula be reorganized to produce better results in science, languages, and specialized training? How can teachers' salaries be raised and better teachers secured? How can the brightest students be selected and channeled through higher education? How can the colleges and universities function more effectively as citadels of learning—scientific and humanistic?

Senator Fulbright, author of the legislation providing for the Fulbright aid for foreign studies and himself a former Rhodes scholar, appropriately gave to the Senate his mature judgment on methods of dealing with education in the current crisis. He is a speaker at ease both in prepared manuscript delivery and in off-the-cuff extemporization.[10]

[8] Text from the *Congressional Record*. 104:797-804. January 23, 1958 (daily edition). Text and permission for this reprint supplied through the courtesy of Senator Fulbright. For excerpts from the speech see also New York *Times*, January 24, 1958.

[9] For biographical note, see Appendix.

[10] For further comment on Fulbright as a speaker, see *Representative American Speeches: 1951-52*, p60-5.

Relatively bleak internal conditions of Russia may, in fact, have the effect of inducing the people of the Soviet Union to work all the harder. In the case of the young, especially, it may induce them to exert every effort to achieve an excellent education —this, because they know that if they remain uneducated, they are doomed to live at a bare subsistence level.

It is, in fact, precisely in the field of education and basic research that the Russians have apparently made their greatest progress. Why should this be so? How is it that they recognized some years ago that trained minds were indispensable to modern technology, modern weapons, and modern methods of subversion? How is it that they had the vision to upgrade the pay and status of educators and scientists to a level just below that of the ruling hierarchy itself?

It may be that the scholar in the field of history or politics is restrained by Communist dogma. But it seems fairly clear that the Communists have had the good sense to give way whenever there is conflict between their doctrines and the physical sciences. Witness the results they have achieved. On the other hand, there is little evidence that the scientists and professors are unhappy with their lot in the Soviet Union. Very few, if any, of them are found among the refugees who seek asylum in the West.

So once again the question intrudes itself: Why is it that Soviet leaders, for all their roughness and brutality, have had the shrewdness to recognize the supreme importance of education? Why is it that a system of government which we are told has many inherent weaknesses and is threatened by present internal stresses and strains, has had the foresight to take the long view and to devote a major effort to education?

This determined and successful drive by the Russians to cultivate to the utmost the intellectual powers of their people is the most serious, the most difficult challenge of all to meet. It will require leadership of the highest order, with vision and persistence over the long term. Our people, and our political leaders, react promptly and decisively to a challenge requiring a short-term, tangible solution, such as more missiles or submarines. They have been somewhat less successful in pursuing long-term policies, thoughtful and discriminating in concept, and intangible in character.

The question intrudes itself, and we can answer, in part, that the Soviets inherited from the old Czarist government a tradition of intellectual excellence and scientific curiosity going back to Peter the Great and the founding of the Academy of Sciences at a time when America was still a wilderness inhabited by savages. Yet the greater part of the answer, so it seems to me, lies elsewhere.

It lies in the fact that the principal rulers of Russia are professionals who have spent their entire lives in governmental affairs. Their past and their future, their personal fortunes as well as their political positions, are identified with the strength and success of the government of Soviet Russia. The facts here are documented by Milovan Djilas [a former Communist party leader in Yugoslavia], who, in his recent book, *The New Class,* emphasizes the proprietary nature of the relationship of the Communist party with all the resources of Russia.

To repeat, the members of the party, and especially the leaders of the party and the rulers of Russia, own the place. None of them regard their sojourn in Moscow as a temporary sacrifice to the public welfare. They hope and expect to be in Moscow for a long time. They have no comfortable corporate berths to which to retire. They are interested in strengthening the power and endurance of their government because it is the same as strengthening their own power.

In other words, there is an identity of interest between the government, as such, and those who control and operate it. And as they have every reason to take the long view in matters of national policy, they have every reason to encourage Russian scientific and technological developments—since it will be the New Class itself which will get the first benefit from what that science and technology produces. . . .

On the grounds just set forth, then, it does not seem that we ought to count on any easy salvation such as might be produced by Russian internal developments. If we are to survive as a nation and as a democratic society—and if the West is to survive with us—it will be through what we do, and therefore force the Russians to do, and not through what the Russians on their own do or fail to do.

Where, then, do we now stand? . . .

Right now, even in the hour of our so-called awakening to danger, the evidence offered by the Administration that it is alive to the most difficult of all the challenges we face is discouraging in the extreme. There is little doubt that we will meet the immediate problem of missiles and satellites. But the real challenge we face involves the very roots of our society. It involves our educational system, the source of our knowledge and cultural values. And here, the Administration's program for a renaissance of learning is disturbingly small-minded. . . .

There will be those among us who will say—"but education takes too long, and we do not have the time; our efforts must be devoted to missiles and outer space." This is truly the counsel of despair and disaster. The start toward improvement in education must be now; it should have been yesterday.

Our most pressing short-range objective should be to start now on our long-range programs. The Administration's proposal of a scholarship and counseling program of $250 million a year for four years is a step in the right direction. To that proposal there should be added an additional authorization for $500 million a year to be distributed in accordance with the formula of Senate Bill 472, approved by the Senate by a vote of 58 to 22 in 1948. This would make a respectable start toward our goal. . . .

Not only should we provide more money for education as a whole but we should also reform our basic ideas about elementary and secondary education. We must emphasize the rigorous training of the intellect rather than the gentle cultivation of the personality which has been so popular in recent years.

If we are to play the role of a leader among nations, in truth if we are to retain our independence, we must have men and women who can read, write and speak effectively and who understand thoroughly the world in which we live. Courses in life adjustment and co-ed-cooking will not do the job. Mathematics, languages, the natural sciences and history must once again become the core of the curriculum, and a way must be found to induce the students to study, preferably by inducing a desire to learn. Intellectual discipline is essential to our purposes.

The lesson of Sputnik, to me, is not merely that we have fallen behind in a significant scientific field, important as that may be. What is more significant is that we have failed to appraise honestly and dispassionately the strength of our adversary and the weakness of ourselves. Either we have failed in this appraisal, or, if not, we have been so blind and satiated with our luxury and our slogans that we are unwilling to admit that which reason tells us must be true.

Whether it is a failure of knowledge or of will, it has, so far, been a failure to cultivate properly the very element on which our society fundamentally rests—the proper education of its people.

If our own choice is for the good life, while we remain indifferent to the rigorous conditions on which the good society can be attained, then our leadership will itself beguile us by promises of a good life. But if we ourselves acquire wisdom, if we ourselves become concerned about the good of the whole, then sooner or later the kind of leadership we cast up will itself mirror our own resolution to get on with the job and stay at it.

Where are we? We are in serious trouble.

Whither are we tending? We are tending toward national disaster—unless important and drastic changes of policy in many aspects of our domestic and foreign affairs, make a true revival of learning the wheel that makes all the other wheels turn.

Do we have time? We will never have more time. Long years ago it was said: "Civilization is a race between education and catastrophe."

RELIGION

A NATION UNDER GOD [1]

EDWARD L. R. ELSON [2]

The Reverend Edward L. R. Elson, President Eisenhower's regular
pastor, gave this sermon in the National Presbyterian Church, Washington,
D.C., on the occasion of the Second Inauguration of the President and
Vice President Richard M. Nixon, on Sunday morning, January 20, 1957.

The President and Vice President, accompanied by their families,
joined in this pre-inaugural servce at nine o'clock, at the President's
church, six blocks from the White House, on Connecticut Avenue. The
service and sermon were keyed to the brief White House ceremony to
take place shortly before eleven o'clock.

The text and discourse itself were in harmony with the ceremonies
of the day and those of the formal inauguration program twenty-four
hours later. The text and scripture passage in Psalm 33, for example,
were those on which the President's left hand would later rest when he
took the oath of office.

Dr. Elson stressed the concept of God as the central tenet in
America's political life. National destiny under God is a matter of
personal responsibility. "Freedom is always one generation away from
extinction," declared the speaker. His plea was that America should be
"a citadel of man's true freedom and a vast bastion of spiritual power."

Although little was theologically original, the sermon served as a
highly appropriate introduction to the oathtaking one hour later at the
White House. In the presence of some eighty relatives and close friends
of the President and Vice President, Senator Knowland administered the
oath of office to Vice President Nixon, and Supreme Court Chief Justice
Earl Warren to President Eisenhower. This Sunday ceremony prevented
any gap between the expiration of the previous term of office and the
extended ceremonies of the next day.

Dr. Elson is a dynamic speaker. On less formal occasions he
extemporizes well with little reference to a manuscript.

Blessed is the nation whose God is the Lord.—Psalm 33:12

"In the beginning God." On these first words of the Bible
early America staked down its life.

[1] Text with permission for this reprint furnished through the courtesy of Dr.
Edward L. R. Elson. For text see also *Congressional Record*. 103:591-2. January
29, 1957 (daily edition).
[2] For biographical note, see Appendix.

This central tenet of our life was explicit in our Declaration of Independence. It is implicit in our instruments of government. It permeates our institutions. And it is manifest in our common days. The virtues of our people and the values in our culture are derived from the premise that this is "one Nation under God."

This basic truth has been mediated to our people through many religious traditions and by many denominations. All espouse in common a faith in a transcendent God in history and beyond history. In some this faith in God has been intimate and personal; in others an attitude of life derived from the social climate and the cultural atmosphere produced by religious faith, principally evangelical Christian faith.

To be sure, America has as a principle the complete separation of the institutions of the Church from the institution of Government. In our plural religious structure, this separation has been a source of virility to both Church and State. But while we cling tenaciously to this principle of separation, no doctrine of American life has ever or ever will eliminate or minimize the presence, the power, or the influence of religion in our national affairs. Religion and national destiny are forever intertwined.

To be "under God" is to acknowledge that this is God's world—that He is the sovereign Lord and Ruler of all life. He is the God of Creation. Man, created in His image, bears some of God's characteristics. Man is a person as God is a person; and the only reason for treating human beings with dignity and respect is that they are *persons* created in God's image, with immortal souls and an eternal destiny. Thus created by God in God's own image, man is free under God's rulership. His freedom is God-bestowed, not an attainment but an obtainment. Man is born free and the chief end of this free man as the catechism long ago said is—"to glorify God and enjoy Him forever." God Himself is the Lord of Creation and He will have no other gods before Him. Therefore, that nation which deifies itself, or absolutizes some reality in its life cannot be a nation "under" God. Such is idolatry for that nation has usurped God's place. Americans have rejected this temptation. Americans believe God is above the nation.

To be "under God" is also to be under His Providence. There is a destiny for that nation whose "God is the Lord"—a destiny shaped and determined by the Almighty Himself. Our spiritual forebears covenanted with God, not as a tribal or a racial deity but as the universal God, who while being the God of all people, becomes in a special sense the God of those who accept His purpose for human life.

Our history has meaning only in these terms. We are a people under God's Providence.

To be "under God" is to be guided by Him. That nation which seeks to understand and obey His laws; that nation which seeks to discern and do His will—only that nation becomes an effective instrument of God's purpose on the earth. Above all, over all, guiding all, empowering all is the transcendent God. To the degree we possess His mind and spirit which is at the center of the universe, and which we Christians believe to be revealed by Jesus Christ, we are and we shall remain a "nation under God."

This concept of freedom under God cannot survive as a mere intellectual expression. Apart from its Source, it will wither and die. But enriched by prayer, strengthened by worship, maintained by a variety of spiritual disciplines, our great nation can successfully confront all forces which would corrupt its life or destroy its freedom. A dynamic and witnessing faith is not an option for our time; it is an imperative for all ages.

But deeper than these truths, a nation "under God" is a nation under God's judgment. God is sovereign Ruler of a moral universe. Man is not the final source of values. Nor is the nation the highest tribunal of judgment. The values by which both men and nations are judged are eternal. They rest with God. They inhere in His character. Man and his institutions are under God's final judgment. There is a divine order above all and beyond all, in time and beyond time, where love and justice and righteousness and truth are absolute—the perfect order of God's Kingdom where God rules the heart and conscience of all beings. There is a higher court of Judgment above all persons, above all nations, above all cultures, even above all universes—the Court of God's eternal perfection. A nation "under God" is always under His judgment.

Here in this capital city this truth was legislated into our Pledge of Allegiance, is printed on our postage stamps and impressed on our coins.

Now let us each impress it deep within our own hearts and manifest it in our lives and national conduct. Such testimony, to be sure, will sharpen the irreconcilable differences between the two great poles of power in our world today. But it will also give us the strength to live in these times and play our God-appointed role in history.

Our dominating concern in Washington on January 20, 1957, is not what we know, not the skills we possess, not the wealth we have accumulated but rather the spirit we convey to the world. To whom are we committed? By whom are we led? These are the commanding questions.

Freedom under God is not permanently secured, nor safely installed anywhere without personal responsibility and unceasing vigilance. Freedom is always only one generation away from extinction. Freedom must be won, understood, guarded and enriched in each age.

Not out of fear, or insecurity, or a substitute for solid thinking; not as an escape to an easy and comfortable way do we seek to reclaim our ancient heritage. But rather we worship and pray, we trust and obey, because it is the very life-spring of our national being.

On days such as this I like to think of our spiritual kinsman, the pioneer American who faced the frontier and the future with three implements in his hand. He carried an axe, a gun, and a book. With the axe he felled the trees, built his home, his school, his church. With the gun he provided meat for his table and protection from the predatory forces about him. The Book was the center of religious devotion, the textbook of his education and the inspiration of his institutions.

Today's American no longer carries the axe, the gun, the Book. His axe has become America's gigantic industrial machine, and the world sees that. His gun has become America's powerful armament, and the world knows it well. His Book, by the power of the Person revealed therein, is pouring forth the light of a new spiritual birth, and the world must clearly see that.

If we are to lead in this hour America must become a citadel of man's true freedom and a vast bastion of spiritual power, the light of which shines in American lives so brightly at home it will illuminate the dark places of all mankind.

Rightly do we sing:

> Our Father's God, to *Thee,*
> Author of Liberty,
>   To *Thee* we sing
> Long may our land be bright,
> With freedom's *holy light;*
> Protect us by *Thy might,*
> *Great God,* our King.

GOOD FAITH [3]

EUGENE CARSON BLAKE [4]

Dr. Eugene Carson Blake, President of the National Council of Churches of Christ in the United States of America, gave this sermon at the opening session of the National Council of Churches' fourth General Assembly at the Kiel Auditorium, St. Louis, on Sunday evening, December 1, 1957.

Some eight hundred national leaders wearing ecclesiastical robes and carrying banners marched in a procession which opened the six-day assembly. They were part of the two thousand delegates representing thirty constituent Protestant communions with some 37 million members.

Dr. Blake delivered his sermon from the giant stage of the auditorium behind a candle-lit altar. Behind the platform was a huge gold cross.

After the worship service 150 singers of the St. Louis Bach Society and the St. Louis Symphony Orchestra presented Bach's "Magnificat in D Major."

Dr. Blake followed the conventional sermonic method of using a text, and of stating his theme, "Love believes all things."

The problem, to the speaker, lay in the wide distrust that exists in the church—between liberals and conservatives, between different geographical, racial, political, economic, social and other elements within the congregations and denominational leaderships.

The speaker suggested the causes of this distrust and skepticism— causes that lie in the current psychological analysis of human motives. He presented his constructive proposal of exercising mutual faith without gullibility.

The address was almost entirely persuasive, without doctrinal emphasis. The appeal for mutual faith and fellowship, despite the centrifugal influences, might have been even more decisive had the speaker concentrated in his later sections more fully on the positive program for religious solidarity. The sermon, nevertheless, was interestingly developed and delivered. It no doubt achieved religious homogeneity among the communicant-delegates.

Text: I Corinthians 13:7. Love believes all things.
Scripture Lesson: I Corinthians 13.

We live in a technical age and in a complex society. Too easily the analysis of the multiplicity of our problems and the

---

[3] Text and permission for this reprint furnished through the courtesy of Dr. Eugene Carson Blake.

[4] For biographical note, see Appendix.

development of techniques to try to handle them preempts so much of our time and energy that even in a church or a council of churches the essentials of faith and good faith are pushed away from the center of attention and concern.

Tonight at the beginning of this Fourth Assembly of the National Council of Churches, I want to direct your attention to a matter so central that I trust the sermon may have some clear and simple application to all of us whether in connection with our homes and business, our churches and communities, or in the great National Council of Churches which has brought us here this night.

My text is found in I Corinthians, Chapter 13, verse 7: "Love . . . believes all things."

In the familiar analysis, by the Apostle, of the various attributes and aspects of Christian love, *caritas,* or charity, there appears this statement: "Love believes all things." One's first response is, how can love be so blind? In the face of human duplicity, how can love believe all things? Does this not appear to be an example of sentimental idealism which forgets the grim reality of the human situation, which forgets the fact of sin, which asks us to believe just for the sake of believing?

First of all I would remind you that this my text is only a part of the analysis of love. After having made the flat and clear statement that nothing is so important in the Christian Church, whether faith to move mountains, or a martyr's courage, or a prophet's inspiration, or a sage's wisdom, or a scholar's knowledge, the Apostle then in highest poetry makes concrete for action this love which so easily does become sentimentality. He reminds us that love is patient and kind; that it is neither jealous nor boastful; that it is neither arrogant nor rude. Love does not insist on its own way; it does not give way to irritation or resentment. Love does not take pleasure in others' failures, but in their goodness. And then in climax the Apostle wrote: "Love bears all things, believes all things, hopes all things, endures all things."

Tonight out of the richness of the Apostle's analysis of the central motive of the gospel, love, I wish to center your attention on just this one aspect of it—"love . . . believes all things."

I do this because I am concerned that of all the failures and weaknesses of the Christian Church, there is none today more costly to our cause than lack of faith in one another. This may be partly because of the rise in our time of a general knowledge of psychology which has taught us all not to take too seriously the conscious surface view of mind or motive, whether that of others or of ourselves. We have been taught for example to recognize that arrogance may be a mask for a feeling of inferiority, or more happily that a rough exterior often covers surprising softness.

This psychologizing tendency of our time has made everybody more skeptical and much more ready to suspect or charge hypocrisy in others even though there does not seem an equal willingness to recognize hypocrisy in ourselves. The chief result of this new psychological insight seems too often to have persuaded us to accept as a fact that most people are hypocrites, but further, since most hypocrisy is unconscious we have had to learn to live with it.

This general skepticism of one another, and our accommodation to general hypocrisy finds its worst expression and illustration in politics, but in even our churches and especially in such a large Christian organization as the National Council of Churches, it also appears with blighting and crippling effects.

Nobody is much shocked by the duplicities and hypocrisies contained in most political speeches at election time. We are not surprised when a known pagan calls upon God in the climax of his oration, nor do we vote against him on this account. It is all part of the game! We have calloused our minds and hearts to all this just as we can look at a soap or floor wax commercial on television without being really bothered by the fact that most of the personable young men and women must be lying since their sales pitches contradict each other so directly.

Carl Jung in the November [1957] issue of the *Atlantic Monthly* writes: "The question of human relationship and of the inner cohesion of our society is an urgent one in view of the atomization of the pent-up mass man, whose personal relations are undermined by general mistrust." So one of the greatest and most religious of modern psychologists underlines my thesis.

He goes on to write: "Free society needs a bond of an effective nature, a principle of a kind like *caritas*, the Christian love of your neighbor . . . [for] where love stops, power begins, and violence and terror."

What Jung is saying is that any free society must have some voluntary principles of cohesion, Christian love for example, that "believes all things," that has faith in people, else people become masses and ultimately masses must be controlled by the totalitarian techniques of power, violence and terror. . . .

Now let me hasten to assure you that there is danger on the other side as well. Gullibility is not a virtue. When the Apostle wrote: "Love believes . . . all things," he did not mean to be taken literally. There is a place in world politics, in the local community, in the church, yes, even in your family, for a proper skepticism. A Christian is urged to be wise—even if as harmless as a dove.

No, what the Apostle is saying is that trust and good faith are an essential part of good human relationships. The point is that it is as fatal to believe in nothing and no one, as it is to believe in everything and everyone. And if you are forced to choose, it is better to believe and be disappointed than to disbelieve and wound the person, for distrust is a contagious disease which cripples those who indulge in it and destroys at last all community and communion.

This is the key long-range problem of world and national politics. . . . Tonight I shall not take time to develop my theme on the political side except to say that the free world faces a true crisis in that it will be as dangerous to continue 100 per cent skepticism of totalitarian communism as it would be to believe all the protestations of peaceful intentions that come from the Kremlin. Our only long-range hope must be that God is powerful enough somehow some way to convert the Communists. And while we work and pray for that we must pray that the free world's actions may be good enough and wise enough that God may be able to bring to us his renewal and salvation rather than His judgment.

In any case we all would agree, I am sure, that within the Christian Church and churches things ought to be radically better and different. But distrust of one another in the churches—yes, and more particularly in the National Council of Churches— continually threatens the effectiveness of much of the work and witness for Jesus Christ in our nation. I do not need to go into unpleasant and embarrassing detail. All I shall do is remind you that there is distrust between ministers and laity—the distrust goes both ways. There is distrust between ecclesiastical officials and ordinary pastors—the grassroots and the "hierarchies." There is distrust of our conservative constituency by the liberals, theological and political and the opposite. There is distrust between North and South, Eastern seaboard and Middle West, between white and black, between thinkers and doers, activists and mystics, catholic and evangelical, liturgists and free worshipers, rich and not so rich, managers and laborers, owners and wage earners, old and young, men and women.

And there is enough of this mistrust among all these persons and groups of persons so that often our ears are deafened to others' insights we need to learn, and our hearts are hardened, and love (which believes) is unable to bind us into the strong instruments for Christ that churches and Council ought to be.

May I emphasize that I am speaking not about differences of opinion or even of important convictions, but of mistrust of the integrity and Christianity of those persons who hold to the differences. So long as a church is a church and not a sect there will be room in it for a wide variety of conviction and practice, and its life should be enriched by the dialogue that continually goes on among its members. Uniformity and monolithic structure would even more be the death of the National Council of Churches. Nobody looks to the flattening out of the rich variety of faith and life that is in our Council. We should rejoice in the many differences and the multiplicity of insights among us.

Ah, but distrust! That is the danger. For as in society generally, so in the Church, as Jung has put it: "where love stops, power begins, and violence and terror." And one aspect of Christian love, my friends, is to believe—to believe not only God and Jesus Christ, but each other too. Good faith as well as faith. Trust and obey—God—of course. But trust one another and learn from each other.

If you attend carefully many of the sessions of this National Council of Churches here in St. Louis this week, you will doubtless hear many statements with which you disagree, some which you may believe are pernicious and dangerous. But I plead with you in your standing for your conviction as I pray you will, you will do so in Christian love, which does not label the other man or woman a hypocrite or worse, but which trusts—"believes . . . all things."

So you will hear Christ speak to you in this fellowship and so our meeting will forge our Council into His instrument, not ours.

FOUR PHILOSOPHIES OF MODERN LIFE [5]

CHARLES E. SHULMAN [6]

Rabbi Charles E. Shulman, of the Riverdale Temple, New York City, gave this address before the Ad-Sell League of Omaha, Nebraska, on February 5, 1957. Delivered before a lay audience, the talk nevertheless grappled with philosophical-religious themes in an appeal to a sophisticated audience. Specific quotations and illustrations supplied clarity and interest.

Although the four postulates of this discourse were by no means novel, their graphic development here gave the composition qualities of well-balanced logical, emotional, and personal proofs. In the handling of cynicism, nihilism, materialism, idealism, and the five American contributions to civilizaton, each theme was developed in such short compass as to suggest that each would well be material for a full-fledged speech. Each concept challenged the listener to seek a thorough examination of his own basic principles in the background of the current world turmoil, and a faith that would "kindle a flame that will light up the fires of democracy everywhere on earth."

Rabbi Shulman had high school speaking experience in a "Debating English" course in Cleveland, Ohio, a course in which great speeches were memorized and delivered. In his seminary training at Hebrew Union College he had special training in delivery under Miss Cora Kahn, and also experience as a student preacher. His legal training taught him methods of briefmaking that helped with "three-dimensional preparation and writing of sermons." His every speech and sermon for a quarter of century has been written in full. He speaks, however, from "half a dozen three-by-five cards." He "never reads publicly from a manuscript." The Omaha address was carefully prepared, but delivered from brief notes. With him communication with an audience has always been paramount.[7]

This period of world's history which the poet W. H. Auden has called "The Age of Anxiety" has had its effects upon American citizens. We cannot live in a world of confusion and tension without being disturbed by the course of events. Some of the effects on Americans indicate that they may have forgotten

[5] Text supplied through the courtesy of Rabbi Charles E. Shulman, with permission for this reprint.

[6] For biographical note, see Appendix.

[7] Letter to this editor, December 30, 1957.

the paths their fathers trod in the search for adequate living. They are seen in the things we value, in the thinking we do, in the manner in which we view our world, in the purpose or lack of purpose in our lives, in the kind of gods we serve, in the way we face the nations across the seas.

We do not lack bread in America. Nor shelter. Nor comfort. Our standard of living is the highest in the world. Our basic problem in these times is not economic—not when over sixty million Americans are employed and our national income is well over four hundred billion dollars annually; not when business flourishes and trade unions are firmly established and respected. These signs of well being are physical ones. They might be called evidence of the quantitative character of our American civilization. But these external symbols of national development cannot hide some of our present deficiencies. The richer we get the more tense we become, the more insecure we feel. Here we are, wealthier than ever before, more powerful than ever before, yet we devote less and less of our great wealth and concern to public welfare. Our national income rises, our stores are filled with gadgets and staples of life, our consumer goods are enormous in quantity. But our schools are more crowded and dilapidated. Our teachers are more weary and underpaid. Our playgrounds are more jammed and dirty. Our national parks are more neglected. Our law enforcement bodies are more overworked. And we wonder why we have more prejudice, more selfishness, more juvenile delinquency than formerly.

We have physical abundance—houses, automobiles, televisions and frozen foods to suit every conceivable taste. But our spiritual problem is greater than it was a generation ago. We are desperately looking for peace of mind, peace of soul, peace of heart and peace of all else; we are buying popular religious books by the thousands to give us the inner security we so badly need. We definitely need to better the quality of our lives to match our physical quantitative blessedness and to teach us how better to use our gadgets of the new atomic age. We need aid of the kind that will help us be a noble influence for freedom and justice and decency both in our wonderful country and in lands abroad. It is high time that we went beyond the necessities of living which our national abundance offers us so well, beyond the physical preoccupation with a job, a square meal, a new suit of clothes, an automobile and a house in the suburbs, and thought some about individual dignity and individual character in our society in this period when we tend to become indifferent to our neighbors' existence. It is time we added some vision to our life, that we remember clearly that where there is no vision the people perish.

Our real problem in this period of physical change in our living due to wonder drugs and airplanes that fly fifteen hundred miles an hour and television and hydrogen bombs in a shrunken world is to know what to do with what we have, to help others to live so that this abundant physical life may be shared more, to emphasize the things of the spirit that have been so greatly neglected in recent years, to turn our minds to the primary purpose of our existence, to develop individual and national character. We must think more about such things as education and religion which stress intelligent and noble living and turn our gaze on such individual and social needs as more equal opportunities for minority groups, better planning for our cities and suburbs, slum clearance, decent housing, improvement of life for the sick and the aged, a sense of justice toward people abroad who long for the good life we possess and the necessity of helping democracy in other places on earth. Let us face up to our responsibilities as free people. Our treatment of the Negro in this country must sooner or later honor the decisions of our own Supreme Court of the United States if we are to survive as a nation. Our concern for the freedom of Jewish people in the state of Israel must be as important as our respect for the income from Arabian oil and Arabian dictators who purchase arms from the Soviet Communists for war purposes that could conceivably be turned against us. Our interest in Asia must be governed by more enlightened policies than pure trade and commerce if we are to have the good will of the poeple of India and Indonesia and others who can be our friends and allies in making this earth a free world.

If we concentrate only on the material things, if we persist in thinking only of the quantitative factors of our national life that give us physical comfort and pleasure we will forget the warning that one of America's distinguished poets, the late Stephen Vincent Benét, uttered a few years ago:

> You will not be saved by General Motors
> You will not be saved by prefabricated houses
> You will not be saved by dialectic materialism
> You will not be saved by the Lambeth Conference
> You will not be saved by Vitamin D
> You will not be saved by the expanding universe
> In fact you will not be saved!

There are four philosophies in our time followed by men. One of them is cynicism. One is nihilism. One is materialism. And one is idealism. In our brief survey of these philosophies we may be able to see more clearly the causes that underlie some of the confusions and tensions of the day.

1. The philosophy of cynicism is tied to an ancient group called the Cyrenaics, founded by the Greek philosopher Aristippus of Cyrene. Their course was called hedonism—self-indulgence. The end and aim of existence of such people is pleasure. They are indifferent to their neighbors, indifferent to their civic duties, indifferent to world events. Their religion is one of comfort. Their attachment to any cause is only in terms of their own convenience. As free men they will exercise the ballot on election day if it is not raining or if it is comfortable for them to do so. They are not aroused by the social ills of their time. They put their faith in gadgets and more gadgets. Of such people a clergyman, the Reverend Edward Ziegler of Roanoke, Virginia, thought when he rewrote the Twenty-third Psalm in terms of the gadgets of our day (cynic's version):

> Science is my shepherd
> I shall not want
> He maketh me to lie down on foam rubber mattresses
> He leadeth me beside six-lane highways
> He rejuvenateth my thyroid glands
> He leadeth me in the paths of psychoanalysis
> For peace of mind's sake.

Yea, though I walk through the valley
Of the shadow of the Iron Curtain
I will fear no Communist for thou art with me.
Thou preparest a banquet for me
In the presence of the world's billion hungry people.
Thou anointest my head with home permanents
My beer glass foameth over
Surely prosperity and pleasure shall follow me all the
    days of my life
And I will dwell in Shangri-la forever.

2. The philosophy of nihilism. This is a philosophy of power leading nowhere socially or politically. There are individuals who live and dream of naked power for its own sake. They constitute one of the problems of our time because of the shrunken character of the world. And they vitally affect our life and thinking in America because of the instability they can create in the life of peoples. We fought World War II because of this philosophy in Germany under Hitler and Italy under Mussolini and Japan under Tojo. If you would appreciate the consequences of this dreadful philosophy when it assumes authority you can find it in Norman Cousins' evaluation of Hitler's book *Mein Kampf* which was the Bible of Nazi Germany. Cousins tells us that for every word in that book 125 lives were lost in the world. For every page in that book 4,700 lives were lost. And for every chapter in that book 1.2 million lives were lost.

We are witnessing the recrudescence of this philosophy of nihilism in Egypt ruled by a handsome young power-driven dictator, Gamal Nasser, and the dictators of the Arab states who are in league with him. How else can we judge the cynical course of these Arab nations in the Middle East whose rulers turn one face toward the oppressed and illiterate masses and tell them that Communist Russia is their only friend because it is supplying millions of dollars' worth of arms with which to destroy the young state of Israel, who spend millions of dollars of the royalties for oil paid them by the Arabian American Oil Company to set up antidemocratic and anti-Semitic propaganda agencies in the United States accusing my people of double loyalties in their American citizenship because they sympathize with their brethren in the state of Israel and help them in their needs and guide them in their difficulties? The second face these Arab dictators turn to America and to the free world and piously claim that they have bought arms from the Communists to protect themselves against the tiny state of Israel. But if you make a pact with the devil you will not easily escape from the clutches of the devil. Communist Russia does not grant favors without demanding something in return. And the Arabs with their philosophy of Nihilism enjoying their power and their new toys of destruction will awake one day to find they are puppets of Soviet Russia.

3. The philosophy of materialism. This is the twisted heritage of Karl Marx that today rules half the population of the earth—in Russia and its satellites in China, in Indo-China, in parts of France, and Italy, in North Africa and in the Mediterranean. What is it that Marxism stands for?

Its philosophy is that the history of all existing society in the world is the history of class struggles, freeman and slave, patrician and plebeian, lord and serf, guild master and journeyman, oppressor and oppressed—all carry on perpetual warfare. Also: the production of the immediate requisite material means of existence and therewith the extant economic development phase of a nation or an epoch constitutes the foundation upon which the state institutions, the legal outlooks, the artistic, even the religious ideas of those concerned have been built up.

The trouble with this philosophy is that it fails to account for the obvious differences between people which are in the same stage of economic development. It leaves out of account such vital factors as race, religion and nationality. It does not reckon with the vast importance of human personality. It is doubtful whether a single historical event could be interpreted in terms of this theory.

But this philosophy of materialism has been buttressed by dictatorship and slavery and oppression and cruelty and violence and bloodshed. The state as an octopus has swallowed the individual. The dictator is supreme. The few rule the overwhelming majority and the majority is silenced. The whims of the dictator prevail. One day it is Lenin. Another day it is Stalin. Today it is Khrushchev.

We have learned a great deal about the way in which this philosophy is forced upon people from above. The silent masses can do little about it without suffering torture and death. The dictators will not brook questioning of their course of conduct. When Khrushchev was challenged by the British labor people during his visit to England to release the prisoners who differ with him he grew furious and told the English people to mind their own business. The American Protestant mission of churchmen who just returned from Russia reported to their fellow Americans that the antireligious campaign is not quite as crude as it was twenty years ago, that Mr. Khrushchev has just issued a directive to the Communists stressing the importance of using more subtle means of oppression against all religion in the country. And like the smiles of Khrushchev and Bulganin in their meetings with Western leaders this policy of deceit is all the more dangerous than outright hostility. And now these godless Communists who are so cruel and intolerant of the religions of men are posing as the protectors of the religion of the Arabs, the religion of Mohammedanism in the Near East.

We have a way of measuring the success of the materialistic philosophy of communism as it is practiced by the dictators who rule with an iron hand. That way is through the stories that filter out of the Iron Curtain from time to time. One of them used to be told about the Fascists in the thirties. It tells about Khrushchev coming to a movie and sitting incognito in the back row. Suddenly his picture was flashed on the screen and everyone stood up in salute. Khrushchev sat back enjoying the scene when an usher tapped him on the back and whispered ominously: "Listen, you'd better get up too. I don't like him any better than you do. But better get up. It's safer." Another story concerns the school teachers in Soviet-dominated lands. They have had to postpone the history examinations in all schools and colleges because they won't know the correct answers for a while. Still a third one concerns the classroom where each child was given a picture of Prime Minister Bulganin and told to take it home and hang it in a corner of her home. The next day a little girl appeared with the picture. She had brought it back. "What's the matter?" asked the teacher. "Don't you like Bulganin?" "Oh yes," she answered, "I like Bulganin, but we don't have any corner in our room. We live in the middle of the room." A fourth story concerns a new jet plane that transported a citizen in Russia from Pinsk to Minsk in four minutes thirty-two seconds. The citizen was overwhelmed. He rushed to the home of his friend in Minsk and cried: "What a nation Russia is? What a government! Not only the greatest constitution, the greatest leader, the greatest army, but now we have a wonderful plane that brought me here from Pinsk in less than five minutes!" The friend refused to be impressed. "So you got here from Pinsk in less than five minutes. What good did it do you?" "What good? It enabled me to be the first in line to buy a pack of matches!"

4. The philosophy of idealism. It is the philosophy of the potential in each human being as an individual. It is the philosophy on which this nation, America, was founded and built. Thank God it still prevails in our midst as a guide to us and our children in days to come. So much has been said and written about American shrewdness and inventiveness, American concentration on material things, that it would be good to weigh our national achievements in our brief history on the scales of their true merit.

In the year 1897 Dr. Charles Eliot of Harvard University, one of our truly great educators and the originator of the famous five-foot bookshelf of Harvard classics spoke on America's five great contributions to civilization. He pointed out that under our philosophy of idealism property has never been safer in any form of government, that no people have ever welcomed so ardently the new machinery and new inventions generally, that religious toleration was never carried so far and so universally, that nowhere have the power and disposition to learn been so general, that nowhere has government power been more adequate or more freely exercised to levy and collect taxes, to raise armies and to disband them, to maintain public order, to pay off great public debts—national, state and town, that nowhere has property been so widely diffused, that no form of government has ever inspired greater affection and loyalty or prompted to greater personal sacrifices in supreme moments. This is essentially true of America and American idealism. . . .

America's philosophy of idealism has guided our inventions and our free enterprise. America's moral aspiration has touched and inspired the peoples of the world in days past. We must not forget this as we contemplate our present-day association with the nations of the world—the people who are still free and who look to us as examples of the kind of free men and women they would like to follow if given the opportunity. We must help the world to know better what America stands for. The defense of this great nation, as Norman Cousins has reminded us in a stirring editorial in the *Saturday Review of Literature,* rests today as it did all along, not on arms, but on what we stand for in the world. The first front is the moral front. What other people see when they look at America. The kind of hope that comes to life at the mention of our name. The crisp conception of justice inside America and in our dealings as a nation; any ideas we may have about the pooling of sovereignty in the creation of effective world law—all this is what counts. Military preparedness without it is motion without action.

When we become weary of things, confused by the conflicting philosophies of our time, when we wonder about the future of democracy in a world of such disintegration and tension and change it would do us good to read our immortal American documents once more. Among these is the Constitution of the United States and its famous preamble which says:

We the people of the United States, in order to form a more perfect union, establish justice, insure domestic tranquillity, provide for the common defense, promote the general welfare, and secure the blessings of liberty to ourselves and our posterity, do ordain and establish this Constitution for the United States of America.

The philosophies of cynicism and nihilism and materialism ignore the general welfare. Our problem today and tomorrow is to revive strongly in this nation the conception of the general welfare, a conception that has tided us over many wars and crises in the nearly two centuries of our existence. It was dear to the Founding Fathers of this Republic. It is indelibly stamped in the preamble to the Constitution of this nation. It teaches us under this general welfare clause we have developed from small colonies to the greatest power on earth. But we must heed its instruction. W cannot expect equality abroad to be taught by us if we restrict equality at home. We cannot expect to teach others the blessings of opportunity if we deny it at home. We cannot export democracy elsewhere unless it functions here at home. We must have a fighting faith in our philosophy of idealism as did those who preceded us on these shores. And in God's time that faith will kindle a flame that will light up the fires of democracy everywhere on earth.

LONELINESS AND SOLITUDE [8]

PAUL J. TILLICH [9]

Dr. Paul J. Tillich, now professor of systematic theology at the Harvard Divinity School, gave this sermon before the Federated Theological Faculty, at the University of Chicago, on January 6, 1957.

The sermon is conventional in its use of a biblical text: "When the evening was come, he was there alone" (Matthew 14:23). At that point conventionality ceases. The speaker approaches the problems of Christian theology and the interpretation of biblical doctrines and exegesis from an "existential" and psychological approach. Said Tillich, "I do not think it possible today to elaborate a Christian doctrine of man, and especially a Christian doctrine of the Christian man, without using the immense material brought forth by depth psychology." (See his *Systematic Theology*, 1951.) His approach is thus more psychological than moral or social. He has become the "most discussed Protestant theologian in America." [10]

John H. Randall, Jr., Professor of Philosophy at Columbia University, wrote, "Paul Tillich seems to me not only the ablest theologian of the present day, but also by far the most persuasive exponent of the philosophy of existentialism. His is a first-rate mind."

In the sermon here included Tillich develops the theme that only through contemplation and solitude does man "penetrate into the limits of our being, where the mystery of life appears." In solitude, "the center of our being, the inner self which is the ground of our loneliness, is elevated to the divine center and taken into it."

Such condition, without the losing of our lives, will lead to "genuine communion." "Even love is reborn in solitude. . . . Only the presence of the eternal can break through the walls which isolate the temporal from the temporal. . . . The innermost nature of solitude . . . is the presence of the eternal upon the crowded roads of the temporal."

Dr. Tillich is a German-born philosopher and theologian, formerly a member of the theological faculties of Breslau, Marburg, Dresden, Leipzig, and Frankfurt-am-Main, from which university he was dismissed in 1933. Said Tillich (New York *Post,* May 1, 1940): "I had the honor to be about the first non-Jewish professor dismissed from a German university." He was professor of philosophy and theology at Union Theological Seminary, New York City, from 1933 to 1951.

[8] Text and permission for this reprint furnished through the courtesy of Dr. Paul J. Tillich.

[9] For biographical note, see Appendix.

[10] *Time.* 70:52+. June 10, 1957.

In delivery he has a strong German accent; he is reserved, but direct, simple, warm in his interpersonal relations.

He is the author of some twenty-five books, including two volumes of his projected three volumes of *Systematic Theology.*

"He was there, alone" . . . so are we. Man is alone, because he is man! In some way every creature is alone. In majestic isolation each star travels through the darkness of endless space. Every tree grows according to its own law, fulfilling its unique possibilities. Animals live, fight and die for themselves, caught in the limits of their bodies. Certainly, they appear as male and female, in families, in flocks. Some of them are gregarious. But all of them are alone! Being alive means being in a body—a body separated from all other bodies. And being separated means being alone.

This is true of every creature, and it is true of man more than of any other creature. He is not only alone, he also *knows* that he is alone. Aware of what he is, he therefore asks the question of his aloneness. He asks why he is alone and how he can overcome his being alone. He cannot stand it; but he cannot escape it either. It is his destiny to be alone and to be aware of it. Not even God can take away this destiny from him.

In the paradise story we read: "Then the Lord God said, It is not good that man should be alone." And he creates the woman from the body of Adam. An old myth is used showing that originally there was no bodily separation between man and woman. In the beginning they were one; now they are longing to be one again. But although they recognize each other as flesh from their own flesh, each remains alone. They look at each other and although longing for each other, they see their strangeness. In the story God himself makes them aware of this when he speaks to each of them separately, when he makes them responsible each for his own guilt, when he listens to their excuses and mutual accusations, when he pronounces a different curse over each of them and leaves them to the experience of shame in face of their nakedness. They are alone. The creation of the woman has not conquered the situation which God describes as not good for man. He remains alone, and the creation of the woman, although providing a helper for Adam, has only added to the one human being who is alone another human being who is equally alone, and out of them all the others each of whom is also alone.

But is that really so, we ask? Did not God do better than that? Is our aloneness not largely removed in the encounter of the sexes? Certainly it is for hours of communion and moments of love. The ecstasy of love can absorb one's own self in its union with the other self. Separation seems to be overcome. But after such moments the isolation of self from self is more deeply felt than before, even to the point of repulsion. We have given too much of ourselves and now we want to take it back. An expression of our desire to protect our aloneness is the feeling of shame. We are ashamed if our intimate self is opened, mentally as well as bodily. We try to cover our nakedness as Adam and Eve did after they had become conscious of themselves. Man and woman remain alone even in the most intimate union. They cannot penetrate each other's innermost center. If this were not so, they could not be helpers to each other; they could not have human community.

And this is the answer to the question of why God himself could not liberate man from his aloneness: It is man's greatness that he is centered within himself. He is separated from his world and able to look at it. Only because this is so can he know the world and love it and transform it. God, making him the ruler of the earth, has to separate him and put him into aloneness. Therefore, man can be spoken to by God and by man; therefore, man can ask questions, give answers and make decisions. Therefore, he has the freedom for good and evil. Only he who is alone can claim to be a man. This is the greatness and this is the burden of man.

II

The wisdom of our language has sensed these two sides of man's being alone. It has created the word loneliness in order to emphasize the pain of being alone. And it has created the word solitude in order to emphasize the glory of being alone. In daily life these words are not always distinguished; but we should do so consistently, thus deepening the understanding of our human predicament.

In the Twenty-fifth Psalm we read: "Turn thou to me and be gracious; for I am lonely and afflicted." The psalmist feels the pain of loneliness. We do not know the character of *his* loneliness but we know about the many facets our loneliness can have. We all have experienced some of them.

Most widespread is the feeling of loneliness when those who helped us to forget that we are alone leave us, be it by separation, be it by death. This refers not only to those who are nearest to us, but also to the groups which gave us the feeling of communion, groups with which we worked, groups with which we had social contact, groups with which we had spiritual communication. For many people, such loneliness has become a permanent state and a continuous source of melancholy feeling and profound unhappiness. The sighing of numberless lonely people all over the world and in our nearest neighborhood fills those ears which are opened by love.

And now let us turn to those among us who are surrounded by friends and neighbors, by co-workers and co-citizens, who live in a family group and have the communion of the sexes—all that the others do *not* have! And here we ask: Are they without the pain of loneliness? Is their aloneness covered up by the crowd within which they move? Perhaps this is our own situation and we may be able to give an answer to this question. And this might be our answer: I never felt so lonely as in a particular hour when I was surrounded by people and suddenly realized my ultimate isolation. And I became silent, I retired into a corner and left the group in order to be alone with my loneliness. I wanted my external predicament to match my internal one. Do not minimize such an experience by saying that people often do not feel strong enough to obtain a significant place with a group and that their withdrawal is nothing but an expression of their weakness calling for counseling or psychiatric help. Such people certainly do exist in large numbers, and they need help. But I am speaking of the strong ones who have their place within the crowd and who nevertheless have this terrifying experience of ultimate loneliness. They are aware in a sudden break-through of man's real predicament. Do not minimize such an experience by saying that people often feel misunderstood in spite of their urgent desire to make themselves understandable; and that this gives them the feeling of loneliness in the crowd. No one can deny that there are such people and even more, that they are not altogether wrong; for who is really understood, even by himself? The mystery of a person cannot be dissolved into a neat description of his character. But those who feel always misunderstood confuse the mystery of every person with imaginary treasures they believe they possess within themselves demanding of others that they recognize them. But the others don't, and so they feel lonely and withdraw. They also need help; but let us instead consider those people whose real treasures are great enough to find expression and who are understood and received, but who nevertheless have the terrifying experience of ultimate loneliness. In such moments they break through the surface of their average life into the depth of man's predicament.

Many feel lonely because their love is rejected, although they try hard to love and to be loved. Often this loneliness is self-created. There are people who claim as their right what only can come to them as a gift. They withdraw into a self-chosen loneliness, taking revenge through bitterness and hostility upon those by whom they feel rejected, enjoying at the same time the pain of their loneliness. There are many such persons and they greatly contribute to the growth of neurotic loneliness in our days. They, above all, need help; for they easily become the prey of a demonic force which keeps them completely secluded within themselves. There is also the genuine experience of rejected love. No claim was made, but hope was at work. And the hope was disappointed. A community of love came to an end or never came into existence. Such loneliness cuts the ties with our world, it becomes manifest that we are ultimately alone, and that even love cannot take this burden from us. He who can stand the loneliness of disappointed love without bitterness has experienced the depths of man's predicament in a most radical and creative way.

There are two forms of loneliness which do not permit any cover or any escape: the loneliness of guilt and the loneliness of death. Nobody can take from us what we have done against our true being. We feel our hidden and open guilt as *ours*, and ours *alone*. We cannot make anybody else responsible for what has happened through us. We cannot run away from our guilt, we cannot honestly cover it up. We are alone with it; and it is this loneliness which permeates all other forms of loneliness, transforming them into experiences of judgment.

Above all, this is true of the loneliness in which we have to die. We remain alone in the anticipation of our death. No communication with others can remove this loneliness, as no presence of others in the actual hour of our dying can hide the fact that it is *our* death, and *our* death *alone,* that we die. In the hour of death we are cut off from the whole universe and everything in it. We are deprived of all things in the encounter in which we forgot our being alone. Who can stand this loneliness?

III

Loneliness can be conquered only by those who can bear solitude. We have a natural desire for solitude because we are men; we want to feel what we are, namely alone, not as a matter of pain and horror, but as a matter of joy and courage. There are many ways in which solitude can be sought and experienced. And every way is that of "religion"—if it is true what a philosopher has said, that "religion is what a man does with his solitariness."

One of these ways is the desire for the silence of nature. Here we can speak without voice to the trees and the clouds and the waves of the ocean. They answer without words in the rustling of the leaves and the moving of the clouds and the murmuring of the waves. This can be solitude. But only for a brief time. Then we realize: the voices of nature have no answer to the questions of our mind. Our solitude in nature easily becomes loneliness, and we return to the world of man.

Solitude can be found in the reading of a poem, the hearing of music, the seeing of a picture, the thinking of significant thoughts. We are alone, perhaps in the midst of multitudes, but we are not lonely. Solitude protects us like an armor without isolating us. But life calls us back to its empty talk, its unavoidable demands, its daily routine, its loneliness and the cover it spreads over our loneliness.

There can be no doubt: this is not only a description of man's general predicament. It is also, and emphatically so, a description of our time. Today more than in preceding periods man is so lonely that he cannot bear solitude. So he tries to become a part of the crowd. And everything in our day supports him. It is a symptom of our disease that everything is done by teachers and parents and the managers of public communication to deprive us more and more of the external conditions for solitude, the simplest aids to privacy. Even our houses, instead of protecting the solitude of every member of the family or the group, are built in such a way that privacy is almost excluded. And the same holds true of the forms of communal life in school, college, office and factory. A never-ceasing pressure tries to kill even our desire for solitude.

But sometimes God pushes us out of the crowd into a solitude which we did not desire, but which takes hold of us. As the prophet Jeremiah says: "I sit alone, because thy hand was upon me." God sometimes lays hands upon us. He wants us to ask the question of truth which may isolate us from most men, and which can be asked only in solitude. He wants us to ask the question of justice which may bring us suffering and death, and which can grow in us only in solitude. He wants us to break through the ordinary ways of man which may bring disrepute and hate upon us, a break-through which can happen only in solitude. He wants us to penetrate to the limits of our being, where the mystery of life appears, and it can appear only in the moments of solitude.

There are some among you who want to become creative in some realm of life. You cannot become and cannot remain creative without solitude. One hour in conscious solitude does more for your creativity than many hours of learning how to become creative.

What is it that happens when we are in solitude? Let us hear the few words of Mark about Jesus' solitude in the desert: "And he was in the wilderness forty days, tempted by Satan;

and he was with the wild beasts, and the angels ministered to him!" He is alone, facing earth and sky, the wild beasts around him and in him, he himself the battlefield of divine and demonic forces. This is what first of all happens in our solitude. We meet ourselves, not as ourselves, but as the battlefield of creation and destruction, of God and the demons. Solitude is not easy. Who can bear it? It is not easy even for Jesus. We read: "He went up into the hills to pray. When evening came, he was there alone." When evening comes, loneliness becomes more lonely. We feel this when a single day, or a period, or all the days of our life come to an end. Jesus went up to pray. Is this the way to transform loneliness into solitude and to stand solitude? We should not answer this question too easily. Most prayers have not such power. They make God into the partner of a conversation, useful in *preventing* the only true way to solitude. They go easily from the mouth of ministers or laymen. But they are not born out of a solitary encounter of God with man. This certainly is not the prayer for which Jesus went up to the hills. We had better remain silent and let our soul, which is always longing for solitude, sigh without words to God. And this all of us can do even in a crowded day and in a crowded room, even under most difficult external conditions; this can give us moments of solitude which nobody can take from us.

In the moments of solitude something is done to us. The center of our being, the inner self which is the ground of our aloneness, is elevated to the divine center and taken into it. Therein we can rest without losing ourselves.

And now we have reached the point where we can answer a question which you may have already asked: how can communion grow out of solitude? We have seen that we can never reach the innermost center of another being. We always are alone, each for himself. But we can reach it in a movement which rises first to God and then returns from him to the other self. In this way man's aloneness is not removed but taken into the community with that in which the centers of all beings are resting, and so into a community with all of them. Even love is reborn in solitude. For only in solitude are those who are alone able to reach those from whom they are separated. Only the presence of the eternal can break through the walls which isolate the temporal from the temporal. In one hour of solitude we may be nearer to those we love than in many hours of communication. We take them with us to the hills of eternity.

And perhaps if we ask what is the innermost nature of solitude, we should answer: It is the presence of the eternal upon the crowded roads of the temporal. It is the experience of being alone but not lonely, in view of the eternal presence which shines through the face of the Christ and which includes everybody and everything from which we are separated. In the poverty of solitude, all riches are present. Let us dare to have solitude: to face the eternal, to find others, to see ourselves. Amen.

APPENDIX

BIOGRAPHICAL NOTES

BLAKE, EUGENE CARSON (1906-   ). Born, St. Louis; A.B., Princeton University, 1928; studied at New College, Edinburgh, Scotland, 1929-30; Th.B., Princeton Theological Seminary, 1932; honorary degrees at Princeton, Occidental, Missouri Valley, Beaver, and other colleges and universities; teacher, Forman Christian College, Lahore, India, 1928-29; assistant pastor, Marble Collegiate Church of St. Nicholas, New York City, 1932-35; pastor, First Presbyterian Church, Albany, New York, 1935-40; pastor, Pasadena Presbyterian Church, Pasadena, California, 1940-51; stated clerk of the General Assembly of the Presbyterian church; moderator of the TV program "Frontiers of Faith"; president, National Council of the Churches of Christ in the United States of America, 1954-January 1958. (See also *Current Biography: 1955.*)

CAREY, JAMES B. (1911-   ). Born, Philadelphia; educated, Drexel Institute evening school, 1929-31, Wharton Evening School, University of Pennsylvania, 1931-33; LL.D., Rollins College, 1947; electrical worker, 1929-34; national organizer for the United States, AFL, 1934; national secretary, CIO, 1938-   ; general president, United Electrical, Radio, and Machine Workers of America, 1936-41; president, International Union of Electrical, Radio and Machine Workers (IUE-CIO), 1950-   ; vice president, AFL-CIO, 1955-   , secretary-treasurer, AFL-CIO Industrial Union Department; member of various governmental committees at Washington dealing with labor problems; CIO delegate to international labor conferences, London 1945, Moscow 1946, Paris 1947, Rome 1948; contributor to labor journals. (See also *Current Biography: 1951.*)

DOUGLAS, PAUL H. (1892-   ). Born, Salem, Massachusetts; A.B., Bowdoin College, 1913; A.M., Columbia University 1915, Ph.D., 1921; instructor in economics, University of Illinois, 1916-17; Reed College, 1917-18; associate professor

of economics, University of Washington, 1919-20; successively
assistant professor, associate professor, and professor of industrial relations, University of Chicago, 1920-48; service on many
commissions related to unemployment; Guggenheim fellowship,
1931; member, Advisory Committee to United States Senate and
Social Security Board, 1937; private, advanced through grades to
colonel, Marine Corps, 1942-45; wounded, battle of Okinawa;
awarded Bronze Star for heroic service; United States Senate
(Democrat, Illinois, 1948-   ); member, Phi Beta Kappa,
and other learned societies; author, *Wages and the Family,* 1925;
Theory of Wages, 1934; and some dozen other books. (See also
Current Biography: 1949.)

DULLES, JOHN FOSTER (1888-   ). Born, Washington,
D.C.; B.A., Princeton University, 1908, LL.D., 1946; Sorbonne,
Paris, 1908-09; LL.B., George Washington University, 1911;
LL.D., Tufts College, Wagner College, Northwestern University; began law practice, New York City, 1911; director, Bank
of New York; trustee, Rockefeller Foundation; chairman, Carnegie Endowment for International Peace; chairman, Federal Council of Churches Commission on a Just and Durable Peace; secretary to a delegation, Hague Peace Conference, 1907; captain and
major, United States Army, 1917-18; member, Reparations Commission and Supreme Economic Council, 1919; member, United
States delegation, San Francisco Conference on World Organization, 1945; Council of Foreign Ministers, London, 1945;
General Assembly, United Nations, 1946; meeting of Council of
Foreign Ministers, Moscow, 1947: London meeting of "Big
Four," 1947; United States Senate (Republican, New York)
July-November 1949 (appointed to complete term of Senator
Wagner); appointed counselor, Department of State, April
1950; appointed, with rank of ambassador, to negotiate terms of
peace for Japan, 1951; representative at signing of Japanese
peace treaty, San Francisco, 1951; writer and speaker on inter-
national affairs; author, *War or Peace,* 1950; secretary of state,
Eisenhower cabinet, 1953- . (See also *Current Biography: 1953*)

EISENHOWER, DWIGHT D. (1890-   ). Born, Denison,
Texas; B.S., United States Military Academy, 1915; Army Tank

School, 1921; graduate, War College, 1929; second lieutenant, United States Army, 1915; lieutenant colonel, Tank Corps, World War I; advanced through grades to General of the Army, December 1944; Chief of Operations Division, Office of Chief of Staff, 1942; Allied Commander in Chief, North Africa, November 1942; Supreme Commander of Allied Land, Sea, and Air Forces in Western Europe, November 1943; Chief of Staff, United States Army, 1945-48; president, Columbia University, 1948-52; appointed Supreme Commander of the North Atlantic Treaty Organization, 1950; entered in presidential primaries on Republican ticket, January 1952; elected President of the United States, November 1952; suffered coronary thrombosis, September 1955; reelected President, November 1956; underwent operation for ileitis, June 1956; suffered mild stroke, November 1957; author, *Crusade in Europe,* 1948; *Eisenhower Speaks,* 1948. (See also *Current Biography: 1957.*)

ELSON, EDWARD L. R. (1906-   ). Born, Monongahela, Pennsylvania; B.A., Asbury College, 1928; M.Th., University of Southern California, 1931; graduate study, 1932-33, L.H.D., 1954; D.D. Wheaton College, 1934, Occidental College, 1947; graduate study in Europe and Russia, 1926; Litt.D., Centre College, 1952; L.L.D., Norwich University, 1953; ordained Presbyterian ministry, Santa Monica, California 1930; minister, La Jolla, San Diego, California, 1931-41; pastor, National Presbyterian Church, Washington, D.C., 1946-   ; appointed chaplain, United States Army reserve, 1930; advanced through grades to colonel, 1944; active duty, 1941-46; awarded Legion of Merit, Bronze Star, Croix de Guerre, American Theatre Medal, World War II Victory Medal, German Occupation Medal; Freedoms Foundation award, 1951; member of many major committees and boards of religious and educational institutions; speaker at colleges and universities; author, religious books, including *One Moment with God,* 1951; *America's Spiritual Recovery,* 1954.

ERVIN, SAMUEL JAMES, JR. (1896-   ). Born, Morgantown, North Carolina; A.B., University of North Carolina, 1917; LL.D., 1951; LL.B., Harvard, 1922; LL.D., Western Carolina College, 1955; admitted to North Carolina bar, 1919; law prac-

tice, Morgantown, 1922-   ; licensed to practice before Inter-
state Commerce Commission, Tax Court of the United States,
and United States Supreme Court; representative, North Carolina
General Assembly, 1923, 1925, 1931; judge, North Carolina
Superior Court, 1937-47; associate justice, North Carolina Supreme Court, 1948-54; United States House of Representatives
(Democrat, North Carolina), 1946-47; Senate, 1954-   ; trustee,
various educational institutions; served eighteen months with
infantry in France (wounded in action and cited for gallantry
in action), World War I; awarded Purple Heart, Distinguished
Service Cross, and other decorations; various educational offices,
including presidency, general Alumni Association, University of
North Carolina, 1947-48. (See also *Current Biography: 1955*.)

FULBRIGHT, JAMES WILLIAM (1905-   ). Born, Sumner,
Missouri; A.B., University of Arkansas, 1925; B.A., Oxford
University (Rhodes scholar), 1928, M.A., 1931; LL.B., George
Washington University, 1934; admitted to District of Columbia
bar, 1934; special attorney, antitrust division, United States Department of Justice, 1934-35; instructor in law, George Washington University, 1935-36, University of Arkansas, 1936-39;
president, University of Arkansas, 1939-41; United States House
of Representatives (Democrat, Arkansas), 1943-45; Senate,
1945-   ; author of the Fulbright act setting up grants for
foreign study and research, 1946. (See also *Current Biography:
1955*.)

FUNSTON, GEORGE KEITH (1910-   ). Born, Waterloo,
Iowa; A.B., Trinity College, 1932; M.B.A., Harvard University,
1934; L.H.D., Wesleyan University, 1947; LL.D., University of
Pennsylvania, 1948; other honorary degrees; research staff, Harvard Business School, 1934-35; American Radiator and Standard
Sanitary Corporation, 1935-40; Sylvania Electric Products Company, 1940-44; on leave as special assistant to chairman, War
Production Board, 1941-44; president, Trinity College, 1944-51;
on leave as lieutenant commander, United States Naval Reserve,
1944-46; president, New York Stock Exchange, 1951-   ; member of various advisory boards and boards of directors; member,
Phi Beta Kappa. (See also *Current Biography: 1951*.)

KENNEDY, JOHN F. (1917-   ). Born, Brookline, Massachusetts; student, London School of Economics, 1935-36; B.S., *cum laude,* Harvard University, 1940; LL.D., University of Notre Dame, 1950, Tufts College, 1954, Harvard University, 1956; served in United States Navy, 1941-45, awarded Purple Heart and other military decorations; correspondent, San Francisco United Nations Conference, British election, Potsdam Meeting, 1945; United States House of Representatives (Democrat, Massachusetts), 1947-53; Senate, 1953-   ; author, *Why England Slept,* 1940; *Profiles in Courage,* 1955. (See also *Current Biography: 1950.*)

LODGE, HENRY CABOT, JR. (1902-   ). Born, Nahant, Massachusetts; grandson of the late Senator Henry Cabot Lodge; A.B., Harvard University, 1924; with the Boston *Evening Transcript,* 1923, New York *Herald Tribune,* 1924; member, Massachusetts General Court, 1933-36; elected to United States Senate (Republican, Massachusetts), 1936, for the term ending 1943; on leave as major, United States Army Tank Corps, with the British forces, 1942; lieutenant colonel, southern France, Rhine, southern Germany, 1944-45; reelected to the Senate, 1946; defeated for reelection, 1952; appointed by President Eisenhower United States chief delegate to the United Nations, 1953. (See also *Current Biography: 1954.*)

MORSE, WAYNE LYMAN (1900-   ). Born, Madison, Wisconsin; Ph.B., University of Wisconsin, 1923, M.A., 1924; LL.B., University of Minnesota, 1928; J.D., Columbia University, 1932; instructor in argumentation, University of Wisconsin, 1924; assistant professor, University of Minnesota, 1924-28; faculty of law school, University of Oregon, 1928-30, dean and professor, 1931-44; special assistant to Attorney General of United States, 1936-39; arbitrator for United States Department of Labor, 1938-42; chairman, President's Emergency Board, 1941; member, War Labor Board, 1942-44; United States Senate (Republican, Oregon), 1945-56; reelected, as Democrat, 1956; member of several national legal and educational committees and boards; member, Delta Sigma Rho, Order of the Coif; author, *A Survey of the*

Grand Jury System, 1931; *The Administration of Criminal Justice in Oregon,* 1932; other legal publications. (See also *Current Biography: 1954.*)

OPPENHEIMER, J. ROBERT (1904-   ). Born, New York City; A.B., Harvard University, 1925 (obtained degree in three years), *summa cum laude,* Phi Beta Kappa; Cambridge University, 1925-26; Ph.D., University of Göttingen, Germany, 1927; National Research Fellow, 1928-29; International Education Board Fellow, 1928-29; studied at Harvard University, California Institute of Technology, Leyden, Zurich; assistant professor of physics, University of California and California Institute of Technology, 1929-31; associate professor, 1931-33, professor, 1933-47; director of atomic bomb laboratory, Los Alamos, 1943-45; director, Institute for Advanced Study, Princeton, 1947-   ; chairman, general advisory committee to Atomic Energy Commission, 1947-53. (See also *Current Biography: 1945.*)

SHULMAN, CHARLES E. (1900-   ). Born, Ukraine; LL.B., Ohio Northern University, 1920; University of Cincinnati, 1922-23; Ph.B., University of Chicago, 1924, A.M., 1927; Hebrew Union College, Cincinnati, 1924-27 (ordained rabbi, 1927); admitted to Ohio bar, 1920; law department, New York Central railroad, 1920, Sante Fe railroad, Albuquerque, 1921; rabbi, Johnstown, Pennsylvania, 1926-27; Wheeling, West Virginia, 1927-31; Glencoe, Illinois, 1931-47; Riverdale Temple, New York City, September 1947-   ; chaplain, lieutenant commander, United States Navy, 1943; active duty, Navy chaplain, in this country and with Seventh Fleet, in Southwest Pacific; prominent in leadership of Jewish religious and social organizations; member, national advisory board, Anti-Defamation League of B'nai B'rith; chairman, Bronx Urban League; executive board, Bronx section, National Conference of Christians and Jews; author, *Problems of Jews in the Contemporary World,* 1934; *Europe's Conscience in Decline,* 1939; *The Test of a Civilization,* 1947; other books and articles in religious journals.

STEVENSON, ADLAI EWING (1900-   ). Born, Los Angeles, California; A.B., Princeton University, 1922; J.D., Northwestern

University Law School, 1926; LL.D., Illinois Wesleyan University, Northwestern University, Bradley University; reporter, *Daily Pantagraph* (Bloomington, Illinois), 1924-25; admitted to Illinois bar, 1926; member, Chicago law firms, 1927-41; assistant to secretary of navy, 1941-44; chief, Foreign Economic Administration, Italy Mission, 1943; assistant to secretary of state, 1945; adviser, United States delegation, General Assembly of United Nations, London, 1946; United States delegate, General Assembly of United Nations, New York, 1946, 1947; governor of Illinois, 1948-52; Democratic candidate for President, 1952, 1956; world tour 1953; author, *Speeches,* 1953; *Call to Greatness,* 1954. (See also *Current Biography: 1949.*)

SYMINGTON, WILLIAM STUART (1901-   ). Born, Amherst, Massachusetts; United States Army, 1918; A.B., Yale University, 1923; International Correspondence School; Symington Companies, Rochester, 1923-35; Rustless Iron and Steel Company, Baltimore, 1935-37; president, Emerson Electric Manufacturing Company, St. Louis, 1938-45; surplus property administrator, Washington, D.C., 1945-46; assistant secretary of war for air, 1945-47; secretary of Air Force, 1947-50; chairman, National Security Resources Board, 1950-51; administrator, Reconstruction Finance Corporation, 1951-52; Senate (Democrat, Missouri), 1952-   . (See also *Current Biography: 1956.*)

TILLICH, PAUL JOHANNES (1886-   ). Born, Starzeddel, Kreis Guben, Prussia; student, University of Berlin, 1904-05; University of Tübingen, 1905; University of Halle, 1905-07; University of Berlin, 1908; Ph.D., University of Breslau, 1911; chaplain, German Army, 1914-18; Th.D., University of Halle, 1926; D.D., Yale University, 1940; theological faculty, University of Berlin, 1919-1924, University of Marburg, 1924-25, University of Dresden, 1925-29, Leipzig, 1928-29, University of Frankfurt-am-Main, 1929-33; Union Theological Seminary, New York City, 1933-55; Harvard Divinity School, 1955-   ; minister, Evangelical and Reformed Church; author, *The Religious Situation, The Interpretation of History, The Protestant Era, The Shaking of the Foundations,* and numerous other books and articles. (See also *Current Biography: 1954.*)

CUMULATED AUTHOR INDEX

An author index to the volumes of *Representative American Speeches* for the years 1937-1938 through 1957-1958. The date preceding the title of each speech indicates the volume in which it appears.

Representative American speeches. ~ 1937/38–
New York, H. W. Wilson Co.

v. 21 cm. annual. (The Reference shelf)

Compiler: 1937/38–   A. C. Baird.

1. American orations. 2. Speeches, addresses, etc.   ɪ. Baird,
Albert Craig, 1883–   comp.   (Series)

PS668.B3   815.5082   38–27962 rev 2*

Library of Congress

815.08 **Baird, Albert Craig,** 1883–   comp.
Representative American speeches: 1937-1938-   Wilson, H.W. 1938-

v (Reference shelf)

"An annual compilation of American speeches. . . ₁Represents₁ a
variety of speaking types, such as (a) forensic, (b) legislative or delib-
erative, (c) pulpit, (d) demonstrative and ceremonial (including business, dinner speaking, educational), and (e) radio. ₁Contains brief
biographical notes₁." Prefatory note

1 American orations 2 Speeches, addresses, etc. ɪ Title ɪɪ Series
815.08

58W2159   (W) The H. W. Wilson Company